A History of Preston
in Hertfordshire

by Philip J Wray

**Published by
Berforts Information Press**

ISBN 978-1-910693-05-6

Preface

Len Deighton in his seminal novel, *Bomber,* cautions of the consequences of climbing the rusting steps of a control tower at a disused airfield - "Beware! You may end up writing a book about it". A similar warning should be given to researchers of their family's history.

My passion for family history was fired in January 2002 following the death of my mother - read into that what you will. A zealous convert, I careered around the country, badgering archivists in County Record Offices and grilling bewildered, elderly relatives. I also bought my first computer and grappled with its intricacies. After three years, I had reached the stage when I wanted to showcase the fruits of my research in print – a purely personal exercise, 'for my eyes only'. The result was a 46-page, comb-bound book.

During a visit to Preston I was introduced to an academic who, having an interest the history of the village, offered to read and comment on what I had written. When the manuscript was returned it had been savaged - in the politest possible way! Schoolboy errors of grammar and punctuation were exposed and my fine ideas of presentation, gently repulsed: 'This seems a rather odd and curious way to deal with a brief history of the village. Best omitted, I think.' This experience was a cold douche of reality. Time to re-think my approach!

My direct ancestors had lived at Preston from at least 1751 - and a relative still lives in the village. But I slowly grasped that it wasn't just my *immediate* forefathers who were part of Preston - I was related by blood to almost half of the villagers in 1881. I became intrigued by the life my kin had led in rural Hertfordshire and researched the lot of the agricultural labourer and the straw plaiter. So it was that family history's bigger brother, local history, began to worm its way into my consciousness.

Now I was at a crossroads - should I confine myself to the tree-lined lane of family history or explore the wider highway of local history. It was the 'local history' road that beckoned.

The next decision to be made was how to promulgate the fruits of one's researches – a printed book or a web site? There are advantages of having a web site. It is much cheaper to produce than books; its potential audience is millions; additions and alterations can be made easily as a site is not set in stone and there is no limit to its size. The result was the launching of the *History of Preston in Hertfordshire* web site in August 2007. The response to the web site has been fulfilling. In December, 2014, 20,000 unique visitors were notched up; each month, between 900 and 1,200 'hits' are recorded and (most pleasing of all) the average time spent on each browsed page shows that they are actually being read - either that, or they are inducing a soporific stupor at the computer.

However, the printed page was not entirely forgotten. It was ridiculously easy to break into the field of writing articles for national magazines such as *Family History Monthly* and *Your Family Tree*. Several of my articles were published, including three which featured Preston - the village school, the lost manor of Welei and the Preston History web site. Then in 2013, I produced an A4 60-page photobook of Preston's history. It was written using a desktop publishing program. The pages were photographed and placed onto a photobook template. The result was surprisingly well received. I intended to produce more of the same, for a very limited distribution, but the hoped-for Xmas special prices for Photobooks did not materialise. And so this book evolved.

I had climbed 'the rusting steps....'

Philip J Wray January 2015

Contents

Preface	i
Contents	ii
Map of Preston	iii

The history of Preston

Preston's location and topography; Early historical glimpses of Preston	1
The Doomsday Book (1086) and Preston;	2
Preston and the Balliol family; Dinsley/Preston Castle	3
The Knights Templar come to Preston	4
How Temple Dinsley was established; The birth of Temple Dinsley	5,6
Religious services at Temple Dinsley; The importance of Temple Dinsley; Treasure and the Templars	7
Why the Templars fell from grace	8
The manor of Missenden aka Minsden	9
Introducing the Knights Hospitaller; The occupants of Temple Dinsley from 1312; Preston and the plague (1349)	10
Finding the lost manor and hamlet of Welei	11-14
The manor of Maidencroft; Temple Dinsley from 1350; The Sadleirs – owners of Temple Dinsley (1542 – 1712)	15
Minsden Chapel and the rebellion of Prestoners	16,17
Minsden Chapel in recent times	18
John Bunyan and Nonconformity at Preston	19
View of Temple Dinsley c. 1700; Benedict Ithell buys Temple Dinsley	20
Thomas Harwood inherits Temple Dinsley	21
Robert Hinde at Preston Castle	22
The Dartons at Temple Dinsley	23-25
The Pryors at Temple Dinsley; *Bunyan's Chapel*	26,27
Fire at Temple Dinsley	27
St Martin's Church	28,29
James Barrington-White buys Temple Dinsley; The Seebohms at Poynders End	30
The Fenwicks at Temple Dinsley; Sir Edwin Lutyens designs Preston homes	31
Temple Dinsley before/after Luytens' alterations	32
The G Jekyll rose garden at Temple Dinsley	33
Buildings at Preston designed by Sir E Lutyens	34
Douglas Vickers at Temple Dinsley; The Countess of Carnarvon	35
Princess Helena College at Temple Dinsley; Education at Preston; A new school in 1849	36
Preston's plaiting schools; Preston School, 1873; The new school of 1966	37
The *Red Lion* at Preston Green	38
Preston villagers buy the *Red Lion*	39
The Chequers Inn	40
Strawplaiting	41-43
Crime at Preston - Poaching; Petty theft; Drunkenness; Assault; Highway offences; Domestic strife; Arson, Juvenile crime	44-46
Morality - Pregnant brides; Illegitimacy	46
Movement and mobility	47,48
Lanes and Highways	49
Preston's pound; Beating the boundaries	50,51
Preston's allotments	52
Preston's Benefit Clubs	53
Cricket	54
Preston - best-kept village; Preston Green	55,56
The well at Preston	57

The historic cottages of Preston

Cottages at Preston Green	58
Pryor House; *Fig Tree, Vine* and *'Peters'* Cottages	59
The Old Forge; *St Martin's Place*	60
Cottages east of *Bunyan's Chapel*, Church Lane	61,62
Cottages at School Lane	62
Cottages at Crunnells Green and Wright's Lane	63
Cottages at Back Lane; *Spindle Cottage*; Cottages on north side of Chequers Lane	64
Sadleirs End; Cottages at the junction of Chequers Lane and Butchers Lane	65
Sootfield Green; Estate cottages at Preston	66
Offley Holes Farm; *Offley Holes House*	67
The Dower House aka *The Cottage*	68
Castle Farm; *Pond Farm*	69
Preston Hill Farm; *Home Farm*; *Temple Farm*	70
Affordable 'social housing' at Preston; Chequers Lane; Swedish Houses, Templars Lane	71

Selected events at and people of Preston

Preston men who fought in the Great War	72-77
Preston and World War Two; The Menace from the sky; Of soldiers based around Preston; 'The Evacuated' come to Preston; Land Girls, POWs and youth workers; Of food and rationing	77-82
The Preston Hill 'murder' (1864)	83,84
Mary Woodhams and Preston School	84,85
The Wallers - builders of Preston	86,87
Nina Freebody - historian	88
Dick Middleditch - umpire and gamekeeper	89
The reminiscences of Robert Sunderland	90,91
Samuel Hall and family	92
The Scotts of Church Lane	93
The Armstrongs and the Newells	94,95
Alfred and Emily Wray	96-98
William (Bill) and Rose Stanley	98
Ann Maybrick and the Preston Scrapbook	99
The Peters family	100,1
Tom Ashton - baker of Preston	102
Flossie Sugden nee Wray	103
Book dedication to Sam and Grace Wray	104
News stories and Preston	105
Acknowledgements, references	106
Index	107,8

Note: This book has been produced for educational and instructional purposes only. A contribution is suggested for the cost of printing and p&p where applicable. No profit is made from its distribution - it is a non-commercial local history publication. More information about Preston's history can be read at the *History of Preston, Hertfordshire* web site (www.prestonherts.co.uk).   © Philip J Wray 2015

Preston's location and topography

Preston is perched on a ridge of the Chiltern Hills. At 143 metres, the village is only ten metres below the highest point of Hertfordshire. As a result, it is not overlooked or dominated by any hills or forests and therefore has a feeling of openness. This is part of Preston's charm. Apart from one vista from the road at Preston Hill, there are no views of lower-lying countryside or towns. The drawback to this sense of spaciousness is Preston's exposure to the bleak easterly winds that whistle in, seemingly unchecked from the east.

The village is about three miles south of the pleasant market town of Hitchin; ten miles north-east of the sprawl of Luton and three miles west of Stevenage. As London is less than forty miles away, Preston is popular with commuters today. Nearby villages include Gosmore and Ippollitts (to the north-east), Kings Walden (south-west), Offley (north-west) and Charlton (north).

The Chilterns are chalk - as illustrated by the view of Kings Plantation *(above)* (or 'Chalk Hill' as it was aptly known) at the bottom of Preston Hill. In some places, such as Kiln Wood, 'brick earth' is also to be found. There is a skim of clay with flints over the chalk *(below)* which occupied many a stone-picker.

The uses to which Preston's fields were put have always reflected the topography. Early crops would not flourish because the land took weeks to warm after the chill of winter. But it was worthwhile to grow root vegetables such as turnips. Summer sowings of wheat, barley and oats were rewarding. The land was also used extensively for grazing sheep.

Hitch Wood, Wain Wood and West Wood are the remnants of more extensive forests that provided fuel and food for families as well as hunting and shooting opportunities for the gentry.

Early historical glimpses of Preston

The village (or more properly, the hamlet) of Preston probably existed before 1000 AD. It did not, therefore, 'grow around the Knights Templar'. Coins dating from the seventh and eighth centuries have been found near what was to be Temple Dinsley, which indicate that there was a community there at that time.

Many scholars agree that 'Prestune' was an Old English (OE) word and that therefore the village predates the Domesday Book of 1086. This was the conclusion of Prof. Tom Williamson who wrote, 'The parish of Hitchin contains four subsidiary hamlets (including Preston) and these, to judge from their names (which are of OE type), were almost certainly in existence at the time of Domesday although not mentioned in it'. He added, 'the priest tun suggests that it was originally the portion of the estate (of Hitchin) reserved for the sustenance of the minster priests'.

With authority, Hitchin historian, Reginald Hine, concurred. He wrote that 'Preston' was 'derived from the genitive plural of the OE word, preost'. This unsurprisingly, means 'a priest'. But then he slides into murkier waters, stating (with a distinct lack of authority) that it *may* refer to (1) a 'tun' where there was a resident priest (which was such an unusual situation as to justify the place-name, 'Preston' being adopted) or (2) a community of priests dwelling beside a church (which was afterwards formed into the Preceptory of the Knights Templar) or (3) an outlying portion of the two hides belonging to the minster of Hitchin referred to in the Domesday Book.

Thus, one may say that the consensus of opinion is that historically the district of Preston had a religious presence that existed before 1000 AD.

As to why a community became established at this location, perhaps the fundamental reason was the easy access to water for households, farmers and travellers from the unusual preponderance of ponds which were in the vicinity.

The water in ponds was an vital part of a village's existence – it sustained the lives of men and beasts. Before wells were sunk, the main sources of water for quenching thirst, washing, laundering and cooking were ponds. Their purity was improved by the filtering of water through stones as it ran off the lanes but they might still be contaminated by animal deposits and the occasional dead cat or rat.

The map above (c 1811) of Preston Green illustrates the number of ponds in the village. They were permanent features and clearly no mere puddles. Later, when farms were advertised for sale, attention was drawn to the ponds on their land. So, when *Preston Hill Farm* was sold in 1848, it was noted that it had three cattle ponds. The prospectus for the sale of *Pond Farm* in 1884 stated that 'there are ponds of water upon the estate, one of which has a spring which has never been known to fail'. When Temple Dinsley was marketed in 1873, a selling point was the 'pond with a never failing supply of water'.

A pond at *Castle Farm* in 2008

'The Domesday Book' (1086)

As noted earlier, Preston is not mentioned in *The Domesday Book* - though there is a reference to the manor within which it lay. But, this has been the subject of much debate among historians.

When attempting to unravel the puzzle about which manor contained Preston, mention should first be made of the grants of land that were made to the Knights Templar after *Domesday* was compiled. Thus, sometime before 1142, King Stephen gave the Templars land **in the manor of Dinsley**. In addition, from 1142 to 1149, Stephen gave more property **in Dinsley** to the Templars. As well as these grants, in 1147, Bernard Balliol gifted the Templars 'fifteen librates (a librate = 52 acres; 15 librates = 796 acres) of my land...**Wedelee** by name which is a member of Hitchin; fields rough and smooth, streams with woodland'.

Concerning this, historian Wentworth Huyshe made these points in 1906:

1) In 1147, a document states that the Templars were given, 'Wedelee by name, which is a member of Hitchin'.
2) In 1185, the possessions of the Knights Templar included Preston which amounted to four caracates (about 480 acres).

Huyshe argued on the basis of this that Wedelee and Preston were one and the same place. Reginald Hine agreed. *The Victorian County History* states that 'Wedelee (was) in Preston', adding that Wedelee was 'a name used elsewhere for Dinsley'. So, it would appear that Preston was in the manor of Dinsley.

This is possibly confirmed, by the erection of the first known local building of note, Dinsley Castle. It was built to the north of Preston, circa 1095, on the site now occupied by *Castle Farm*. As Preston lies between Temple **Dinsley** and **Dinsley** Castle *(see below)*, the village is likely to have been included in the manor of Dinsley. This conclusion is hardly a leap of faith. For centuries Preston was included in the manor of Dinsley.

'Deneslai' is first mentioned in *Domesday*. Professor Skeat asserts that Dinsley is derived from the chieftain Dyne – Dynes Hill or Dynes Lea. However, the Hertfordshire historian, Nathaniel Salmon, states, 'Deneslai might be derived from the Danes Land, who were much in the Hundred of Dacorum and nearer as the Six Hills (in Stevenage) convince me'. JEB Glover attributes the name to 'Dyn(n)e's clearing or wood'.

The following extract is a translation from *The Domesday Book*:

> *King William holds Deneslai. It is assessed at 7 hides (1,680 acres). There is land for 20 ploughs. In the demesne (the Lord's land) there are 3½ hides (840 acres) and 3 ploughs are on it and 19 villeins have 8 ploughs between them and there could be 9 more. There are 7 bordars and 7 cottars and 6 serfs and 1 Frenchman (a settler from abroad, not necessarily French), a King's almsman.*
>
> *Two sokemen (free men) held this manor as 2 manors of Earl Harold in the time of King Edward and could sell. Yet they each found 2 averae and 2 inwards in Hiz; but this was by injustice and by force as the Hundred (Court) testifies. These 2 manors Ilbert held as one and he was seized thereof by the King's brief for as long as he was sheriff as the Shiremoot testifies. But after he ceased to be sheriff, Peter de Valongies and Ralf Tailgebosch took this manor from him and attached it to Hiz because he refused to find the avera for the Sheriff. Geoffrey de Bech, Ilbert's successor, claims in regard to this manor to have the King's mercy.*

The last paragraph simply means that there had been a resolved dispute over who owned Dinsley. On the basis of this information, there were approximately 180 men, women and children living in Dinsley's 1,680 acres, inhabiting around forty houses.

Preston and the de Balliol family

The de Balliol family left their stamp on English cognesci as one of Oxford's colleges bears their name. Guy de Balliol was a French baron who was granted swathes of land in northern England after the Norman Conquest of 1066. In the reign of William Rufus, he was given the manor of Hitchin for his 'good and faithful service' during the Conquest. Between 1130 and 1133, his nephew, Bernard de Balliol, inherited his possessions including Hitchin. As a result the de Balliols were lords of Hitchin for almost two centuries until 1296.

Bernard de Balliol not only built Dinsley Castle at Preston in around 1095 but his Purbeck marble effigy (now resting in a window at St Mary, Hitchin - *shown below*) was found at Temple Dinsley. It is thought that the tomb of his father, Guy, was also at Temple Dinsley.

Dinsley/Preston Castle (built c.1095)

The next historical reference to Preston is of Dinsley Castle. Now and again, there are intriguing historical glimpses of the ramparts of the Castle. Wentworth Huyshe wrote that Guy de Balliol was 'probably often at his residence at the castle at Preston, which I believe, was built by him (circa 1095 when he was granted the manor) close to the Templars' establishment. (As far as it is known there were no Templar castles in the British Isles so it is unlikely that the Templars built Dinsley Castle.) The site of Preston Castle is about six hundred and fifty yards distant from Temple Dinsley'.

Huyshe adds that in 1278 there is a direct reference that the Prior of Wymondley owned the *site* of the Castle which, by this time, was 'either dismantled or completely destroyed' and suggests that the ruins were robbed-out and that its 'stones, bricks and beams may still exist in the old cottages at Preston'. (Perhaps owners of the oldest cottages at Preston might consider dendrospectronological surveys of beams in their homes.) He then nullifies this suggestion by adding that, 'of course, the Castle could have been destroyed by fire'.

Huyshe suggested that Dinsley Castle therefore stood for less than two hundred years. But, probably during its short life it was the focal point of the manor of Hitchin and from it Bernard Balliol would have travelled to worship at the Templars' Preceptory Chapel at Temple Dinsley, where his father's tomb lay in state. He also moots that if this was the case, it is unsurprising that Bernard made his gift to the Templars.

Hine wrote: 'These Balliols belong not so much to the parish of Hitchin and to the castle of Dinsley as to this realm of England.....no cry comes across the centuries from those who rotted in the dungeons of the Balliols...(who) cursed the cruel castle of Deneslai....the castle of Dinsley which, when the Balliols were banished, was brought into ruin and rented by the Prior of Wymondley at a mere 10s by the year'.

Back to Hine: in the chapter of *Hitchin Worthies* that features Robert Hinde, he asserts that there was a manuscript *History of Hitchin* in St Albans' Museum which mentions the remains of Dinsley Castle and a tradition related by Mrs Hinde of Preston 'that in early times, there was a battle there; that one party took their station where Hunsdon Hall (aka *Castle Farm*) is now and the other on Kings Hill and that one party was pursued to Gosmore where a king was killed and buried under a tumulus there. Flimsy confirmation of this story was to be found in the London Guildhall library where EA Downman had lodged some plans (dated 1902) of these earthworks. Hine also reported that 'the keep, bastion and curtain walling' of the original Dinsley Castle could be seen in Robert Hinde's time. There was a 300-feet-deep well at Hunsdon House/*Castle Farm* which was reputedly sunk for Dinsley Castle.

The Knights Templar come to Preston

In the eleventh century AD, devout Christians from Western Europe undertook a long pilgrimage to Jerusalem. Among the revered, holy sites at the city were the Garden of Gethsemane and the tomb of Christ. The pilgrims made their journey to sightsee, worship and ultimately to have their sins forgiven.

However, what was already a gruelling trek became increasingly dangerous and impossible. Jerusalem was in the grip of non-Christian Turkish overlords who blocked the approach of worshippers to the sacred shrines. Pilgrims were attacked – many were slaughtered and others were sold into slavery.

Responding to this hostility, in 1095, the Pope launched a campaign to free the Holy Land from the infidels using soldiers of Christ.

The Crusaders were born. The rampaging knights were later distinguished by the scarlet cross emblazoned on their coats. Within four years of bloodshed the Turks had been ousted and Jerusalem was in Christian hands. The first Crusade of 1099 was a satisfying success for Christians. With the promise of a safer journey, worshippers again streamed towards the Holy City.

But other perils lay in their path: ambushing robbers, marauding Muslim Saracens and voracious wild animals. Matters came to a head in the Easter of 1119 when 300 pilgrims were massacred by Saracens near Jerusalem.

In a reaction to this butchery, nine knights (most, if not all, were French) pledged to protect Christian travellers. The recently-installed King of Jerusalem provided a home for the knights in the Temple and the intrepid few became known as the Knights Templar.

Returning to the field of conflict at Jerusalem, the Templars needed reinforcements and money to wage their war. In 1127, the first Templar Grand Master, Hugh de Payens, after visiting Normandy, crossed the Channel to England and was 'welcomed by all good men. He was given treasures by all...'. He called for people to go to Jerusalem. His recruitment drive was a success. This is the first mention of the Knights Templar in Britain.

The Templars were also brothers in a religious Order who led a monastic life. 'They dedicated themselves to God, taking vows of chastity, poverty and obedience'. The foremost aim of the Knights is debatable: were they monks or warriors? These descriptions may appear paradoxical as monks eschew the spilling of blood. But the Templars viewed fighting infidels as an act of devotion. War was a version of prayer. Their battle was just and righteous as it defended the Holy Church. So, 'onward *Christian* soldiers, marching as to war'!

Their attire was symbolic - they were commanded to wear white mantles and cloaks to show that they had emerged from darkness into the light of purity. The red crosses on their mantles were added later to distinguish them from other fighters. The knights kept their hair short, but they did not shave their beards.

To understand the impact on Preston of the Templars, one should discern their *religious* aspect as this explains both how they acquired their land in the hamlet and also their manner of life there.

How Temple Dinsley was established

As the Templars were a significant religious body, they were granted of land in return for their awarding redemption of sins and absolution to the donors. These awards eased the recipients' consciences and gave them confidence of being accepted in heaven after their death. So spiritual well-being and deliverance were purchased by the gift of land. The gift of Temple Dinsley was a spiritual 'back-hander'.

There is evidence that the Templars had a foothold at Dinsley *before* 1142 and that between 1142 and 1148, there was a flurry of five separate grants to the Templars there:

1142. King Stephen granted rights and privileges (but not land) on the Templars' existing holding at Dinsley. As it was only rights and privileges that were bestowed, it is probable that Stephen had already given some land to the Templars here – remember that Dinsley was in the King's hand, being described as a 'royal manor' in Domesday.

1142. King Stephen *confirmed an earlier* grant of an acre at Dinsley (called Smith Holes) that John Chamberlain had granted to the Templars.

Late 1142, Stephen gave the Templars 40 shillings worth of land at Dinsley as well as two mills and 'the men of the land'.

April 1147. Bernard Balliol gave the Templars fifteen librates of land (780 acres) called Wedelee which was in his manor of Hitchin. This grant took place at a Chapter of the Templars in Paris around Easter-time. Present were the King of France, four archbishops and one hundred and thirty Knights who were 'arrayed in white cloaks' in what must have been breathtaking assembly. Alluding to the practice of smoothing the way to heaven, Bernard declared that, '....for the Salvation of my Soul, I have given...(to the Templars) fifteen librates of my land...Wedelee by name which is a member of Hitchin; fields rough and smooth, streams with woodland.'

April 1147-49. King Stephen confirmed a gift of uncultivated land or waste in Dinsley.

Why did the Templars settle at Preston? Given that Dinsley was a grant, the site's seclusion was the likely reason for the Templars settling there. Preston is high in the Chiltern hills. Even today, there are swathes of local woodland. A millennium ago, the forests were even more extensive. The site nestles in a hollow *(see above, right)* and 'stands at the head of a long ravine that slopes gently toward the east in the direction of Minsden Chapel'.

So, Dinsley was isolated - a most suitable location for a withdrawn monastic order - and it might be borne in mind that Preston had religious roots, as noted earlier. Despite its isolation, Preston was relatively close to London and near the major ancient highways of the Great North Road and the Ichnield Way.

The birth of Temple Dinsley

Soon after acquiring the land there was a preceptory (a cross between a monastery and a chapel) at Preston. Whether this was adapted from the original 'priest's tun' at Preston or built by the Templars is not known. Huyshe writes, 'The chapel would *probably* (my italics) be among the earliest of the buildings to be erected for the fraternity'.

Whatever its background, there was a community and religious house here and thus Temple Dinsley was created. The *Victorian County History* remarks, 'Not much is known about the preceptor, but it was perhaps fairly important'. The first historical reference to 'Dynesle Temple' was in 1294. Its Master or Preceptor was answerable to the Grand Master of Templars. Preceptors at Dinsley included Richard Fitz-John (c.1255), Ralph de Malton (c.1301) and Robert Torvile (1308).

Although there are no plans of the original buildings, if the normal practices of the Templars were followed, there would have been 'a large complex of buildings'. This is certainly what documents convey. The buildings included a chapel, hall, smithy, bake-house and a graveyard.

The brothers were dedicated to prayer, observed their office day and night, fasted and preserved silence. They lived a frugal life with few possessions or comforts. Theirs was a fairly elderly community as the younger men were fighting overseas.

The precise location of the chapel is unknown, but its existence is confirmed by three substantial artefacts. Firstly, the 'battered effigy in Purbeck marble of Bernard de Balliol' mentioned earlier which would originally have occupied pride of place at the Dinsley chapel. Herbert Tomkins describes it as 'a mutilated, featureless effigy'. The figure was re-united with the second artefact, a foot ('part of a sculptured foot bearing chain mail and spur') which was found at Temple Dinsley in February 1899.

A third artefact is displayed at St Martin's Church *(right)*. It is a grave-stone cover, 'carved with a floriated cross that once marked the resting place of a Templar Master'. In 1913, Tomkins added some information about this find: 'Fortunately for me, a discovery was made a few days back which has set others thinking once again of the men who held this manor so long ago. Leaving the village green, I obtained entrance to the private gardens of Temple Dinsley and here lying upon the ground near the house, in a spot shaded by pines and guarded by an effigy of Father Time with his scythe and hour glass, is a large stone coffin lid which was found by some workmen when digging in the grounds. The coffin itself was missing. On that lid is a filial cross upon a rod or staff with a central disc and foliated extremes'.

Tompkins claimed that this specific pattern was among the insignia of the Knights Templar. This discovery reminded him of another find nearby, the 'sculptured foot', which was mentioned earlier. Preston was agog: 'I find no small interest is evinced by them in those stories which they have heard from time to time'.

Tompkins sat by this 'old, old stone' and listened to all that the gardener had to tell him. 'Not far from where I am sitting is the mouth of a subterranean passage. It has been opened, as I am told, from time to time, but never fully exposed. The story runs that it leads from here to Minsden Chapel and that, once upon a time, a second passage ran from the Priory at Hitchin and met that at Dinsley at right angles'.

National Geographic filmed a documentary about the tunnels the Templars built at Jerusalem. So, the Templars *were* tunnellers.

There is also a rumour that beneath Hertford there is a honeycomb of passages dug by the Templars to facilitate their secret movements about the town. R J Pilgram wrote this about Stagenhoe House (which is little more than a mile from Temple Dinsley): 'There has been recurring talk of a secret passage at Stagenhoe to Temple Dinsley. Mr Bailey-Hawkins (owner 1895 - 1922) tried to investigate it with some of his men, but they were driven back by foul air. When Mr Dewar owned the place he stated that he was extremely interested to reach the end of the tunnel, which had collapsed in many places. It seems unlikely that he ever did so. Hine himself did not regard the passage as having any significance. It was moreover a danger and Mr Hawkins car, leaving the forecourt, caused it to collapse.'

However, when describing how the Stagenhoe mansion was underpinned by girders in the cellars, Hine wrote, 'It was when these girders were being installed that a secret passage was discovered leading (so it was said) in the direction of St Pauls Walden Church. It is a pity that it was then bricked up, for speculation as to its course, destination and purpose has been rife ever since. For the most part, one is inclined to be sceptical about such passages...'.

Further evidence of the original Temple Dinsley has been discovered in the form of a few of the floor tiles of the chapel dated from the mid-thirteenth century and embellished with heraldic designs *(see below: left, the Agnus Dei tile; right, the arms of a brother. Images used by kind permission of NHDC Museums)*.

Also, skeletons of monks have been dug up in the kitchen yard. A skull was used by Henry Brand, on his study table as a *memento mori* when he was tenant of Temple Dinsley. Lodged with the bones was a pewter chalice of the early fourteenth century which was discovered in 1887. A fourteenth century bronze jug was unearthed and presented to Hitchin Museum by Mrs Barrington-White.

Away from the main buildings, there were farm structures in the enclosure at Dinsley which confirm that the knights led both a religious and an agricultural life. The Templars also owned a large holding of land at Preston next to Dinsley. Only a quarter of the Templars' land at Preston of land at Preston was held in demense, (that is, set aside for the Templars' own use) and for centuries this was referred to as 'Temple Land'. The rest of the manor was tended by their tenants who were freemen, villeins and cottars (who had a house and a small piece of land and probably worked for the other two classes).

The Templars received further grants of land: 13 acres in Kings Walden, some at Charlton (1244-5 from Maud de Lovetot) and 2 marks rent in Welles at Offley from John de Balliol. They also enjoyed fishing rights on the River Hiz, and free warren (from Henry III in 1252-53) in their demense lands of Dinsley, Stagenhoe, Preston, Charlton, Kings Walden and Hitchin. This enabled them to kill game in those districts. Even in the twentieth century, the Lord of Temple Dinsley still had the right to stand on the steps of Stagenhoe House on Christmas Day and fire a shotgun.

The Templars also had the right to erect gallows. They hanged a man at Baldock in 1277, which indicates that their jurisdiction extended to this district. In 1286, they hung Gerle de Clifton and John de Tickhill for stealing a silver chalice and four silver teaspoons from a Dinsley priest as well as Peter, son of Adam, for taking and torturing a woman.

Religious services at Temple Dinsley

The niece of William the Conqueror, Judith, formed the Benedictine abbey of Elstow, Bedfordshire towards the end of the eleventh century. It was seen as a royal foundation and its property, which included St Mary, Hitchin, was large and scattered. The nuns had the right to appoint a priest at St Mary, Hitchin.

In 1218, the Templars agreed with the nuns of Elstow that they should provide a resident chaplain at Dinsley who would celebrate matins, mass and vespers on Sundays, Wednesdays and Fridays in the morning, followed by vespers in the afternoon. The nuns provided a silver mark each year and four pounds of wax for the candles in the chapel.

The Templars paid for services rendered by the nuns, giving a tithe from all the land that they ploughed in Hitchin as well as any land that was 'newly broke up and sown'.

But if we were to imagine Temple Dinsley as a complex populated by knights in resplendent armour, this would be a mistake. Even Reginald Hine has been criticized for painting a romantic picture in his *Early History of Temple Dinsley*. This was triggered by his observation that there is a meadow close by called Pageant Field. He suggested that 'we shall do wisely, I think, to follow the prompting of that word (pageant)'. He then dreamed of standing on Preston Hill and watching a 'procession of the ages' looming through 'the mists of time and standing in bright armour'.

Evelyn Lord dumped a douche of ice-cold water over this fanciful whimsy – she wrote dismissively, 'Pageant Field did not get this name until 1729........ and holding tournaments would have been against the Order's Rule as encouraging competition and pride'. Do get a grip, Reginald! Rather, Temple Dinsley had the trappings of a trappist-like monastery.

The importance of Temple Dinsley

Temple Dinsley at Preston is recognised as 'the most important preceptory (of the Templars) in the British Isles outside London'. The preceptory 'became the most important in South East England'.

The administration of the Templars outside London was through provincial chapters. By the end of the thirteenth century, these important assemblies were held at Temple Dinsley. Several Chapters (or AGMs in today's parlance) were held between 1200 and 1310. As a result there was an impressive list of visitors to Preston and Temple Dinsley. These included Henry III and the last Grand Master, Jacques de Molay.

Treasure and the Templars

The Templars are often linked with hidden treasure. In the twentieth century, a girl from the Princess Helena College (PHC) was found wading 'up to her middle in the lower pool in the sure and certain hope that at any moment her toes might touch the bars of gold and the fabled iron casket'.

> *Temple Dinsley at Preston is recognised as "the most important preceptory (of the Templars) in the British Isles outside London".*

Hine reported in the 1920s that folk in 'agonies of baffled expectation have been digging for 600 years the buried treasure' that still eludes them. How was this fantasy of buried bullion created?

The Templars evolved a system of banking. This was due to practical necessity – it was simply not feasible to travel any distance, let alone thousands of miles to the Holy Land weighed down with gold - a tempting target for any bandit. So, the Templars evolved a monetary system which allowed money to be transferred between their preceptories *on paper*. As a result, an amount written in France or England could be drawn upon in the Holy Land - it was effectively a credit note. It wasn't just the Templars who needed this facility. Their services were used by kings and noblemen to collect and store taxes, pay ransoms and act as money couriers. The Templars offered a safe deposit service and were trustees for the payment of annuities and pensions. Large deposits of money still had to be carted around, against which paper could be raised and the impression was given that the Templars were incredibly rich to those witnessing this ancient Securicor-like business in transit. They missed the point - the hefty bags did not contain *the Templars'* money – the Knights were mere custodians. They were like the security guard who earns £200 a week and who carries £100,000 into a bank: this is not *his* money. The revenue that the Templars earned was sunk into the bottomless pit of financing their army in the Middle East.

It was this misconception of their part in the banking world that created the fiction of their wealth and hidden treasure. The reality was that they were poor (that is, *financially* poor) monks. When the Templars were attacked in the early fourteenth century, little of worth was found, not because it had been spirited away, but because it had never been. Perhaps this knowledge was included in the curriculum of Princess Helena College to deter further watery treasure hunts. Even the King of England was not immune from enticing rumours about treasure troves. After Dinsley was wrenched from the Templars in 1309, a commission was issued to 'inquire touching goods of the Templars in the county of Herts.' Nothing was found.

In the fourteenth century, believing that possibly Temple Dinsley had a complex of underground passages and buried treasure, Edward III sent a team to Preston to dig for the buried fortune – the foragers were to have a half share of the spoil. Another blank. Wentworth Huyshe describes an intriguing conversation about Temple Dinsley with Mrs Anstruther (who lived at *The Cottage*, Preston):

> *Rumour murmurs a half-forgotten tale of how somewhere in that garden, perhaps beneath the straight grass walks, perhaps beneath the sunflowers and the pansies, the clumps of daisies and of dahlias – somewhere in that garden – lies a wealth of hidden treasure; jewels, rich and rare, rubies and diamonds, emeralds and sapphires and gold and silver galore hidden centuries ago by desperate men whom the King was despoiling of their own.. But the exact spot where that treasure lies, no man wots of today, though some of the old folk in the village babble still of a certain oak tree, so many feet to the eastward of a certain pool; yet despite their babbling it is a fact that whereas men in the course of their daily labour have dug and trenched every inch of that garden, nothing have they brought to the surface, except some human skulls and bones which seem as though the bones of men. But never yet the treasure.'*

Why the Templars fell from grace

In 1291, despite all their battling, the Christian armies were repulsed from the Holy Land. This created a fundamental crisis for the Templars: their essential raison d'etre was non plus pas. Furthermore, the recruitment stream was drying up and theirs was an ageing force. Appropriately, their 'rock' in this time of need was the Pope.

The military problem in the Holy Land was exacerbated because the Christians had splintered into separate armies – each rivals, yet with the same aims. Among the contenders of the Templars were the Knights Hospitaller, who were to feature later at Preston. The Grand Masters of the Templars and the Hospitallers met the Pope in 1306. The two main bullet-points on the agenda were how to merge the two orders and the launching of a new crusade.

However, there was another more influential power struggle brewing. The Pope's authority was being challenged by kings, notably Philip IV of France. As many of the Templars lived in that country they were squeezed between their king and their increasingly weakened protector, the Pope. Added to the cauldron were the jealous glances Philip directed toward the Templars' supposed wealth and his perception that they were religiously corrupt and evil and that he was 'King Right'.

Matters came to a head at dawn on 13 October 1307. Philip ordered the arrest of all the Templars in France. They were accused of terrible crimes: of sodomy, heresy and apostasy. Permitted to torture his victims, some 'confessed' under extreme duress that the charges were true. This gave Philip still greater power to spread his attack abroad.

The Pope issued a Bull or edict against the Templars. This spiritual tsunami created a wave of assaults even in the backwaters of secluded Preston. Despite his reservations, the King of England, Edward II, had no choice but to also arrest the English Templars because of the papal Bull - to ignore it was to put the well-being of his very soul at risk.

Thus, on around 10 January 1307, the rural calm of Preston was shattered by the arrival of the Sheriff of Hertfordshire's men at Temple Dinsley. They seized six Templars and dragged them away to face trial. (Perhaps Reginald Hine would have been on surer ground if he had pictured *this* wintry raid while standing on Preston Hill.) Two of the brothers were taken to the Tower of London and the other four were escorted to Hertford Castle. The known Templars arrested at Dinsley, included Henry Paul, Richard Peitvyn (who had been at Dinsley for forty-two years), Henry de Wicklow and Robert de la Wold.

At the time, there were six other men living as pensioners at Dinsley, together with two priests, (who acted as chaplains) and three boarders. Little wealth was recovered during the raids on Templar property in England.

The manor of Missenden aka Minsden

Lest we become obsessed with the domination of Preston by Temple Dinsley, it is time for a reminder that the districts around Preston were also governed by other manors. One such was Missenden or Minsden.

> *Domesday* reported that 'King William holds Mendlesdene. It is assessed at 4 hides (480 acres). There is land for 8 ploughs. In the demesne (the Lord's holding) there are 2 hides and 2½ virgates. A priest with 8 villeins and 2 cottars have 3 ploughs between them and there could be 2 more. There are 6 serfs. Meadowland there is sufficient for the livestock of the vill. There is woodland to feed 30 swine. The manor belonged and still belongs to Hiz (Hitchin). Earl Harold held it.'

Thus, significantly, a priest lived at Minsden together with around thirty-eight other people in sixteen homes. We might conclude that there was a church at Minsden in 1086 (although Bishop suggests that Minsden Chapel was built in around 1300).

The manor comprised mainly of meadows and included a compact wooded area. Gerry Gingell described it as 'a very small hill-based community which struggled for survival up until the seventeenth century.'

Pictured above is the hilltop of Minsden. The chapel is to the right of the copse. It was a chapel of ease to St Mary at Hitchin and served villagers from the village of Langley. As it lay near the pilgrims' route of St Albans Highway (being clearly visible from the road, perched on a hillside) it also would also attract travelling worshippers who passed by.

Did Prestoners worship at Minsden? As we will see, there is no doubt that they attended services there in the sixteenth century. However, as noted earlier, from before *Domesday* there had been a religious house at Preston and the Templars had established a preceptory at the village from the end of the twelfth century.

Was the preceptory for the exclusive use of the Templars, thus excluding local folk? Probably not - non-Knights (albeit august personages) such as the de Balliol family worshipped at Dinsley.

Perhaps Preston worshippers only drifted to Minsden when regular services at Dinsley were interrupted several centuries later.

Minsden manor was owned by Guy de Bovencourt until the King claimed it back in 1204. Then, Minsden was included in the holdings around Hitchin which rested with the de Balliol family until 1295. Afterwards Robert de Kendale assumed ownership until he was ousted by the King on a point of law – of which possession was not nine points in this case.

In the fourteenth century, Minsden was conferred upon John de Beverle 'for services rendered'. Then, it was passed down to his wife and two daughters. In the early 1400s, the manor was sold to the Langfords - Robert, then his son, Edward, followed by later generations of this family.

We will return to Minsden later.

Introducing the Knights Hospitaller

If anything, the origins of the Hospitallers slightly predated the Templars as their Order was set up in the 1070s. If the Templars kept the routes to the Holy Land open, then the Hospitallers tended those who fell by the wayside. They opened a hospice (as distinct from a hospital) at Jerusalem which ministered to sick and injured pilgrims – they *eased* their plight rather than treating them. They were a quasi-religious Order who took vows, donned distinctive clothing and existed to provide a positive service for others with an emphasis on spirituality.

In 1113, their role was acknowledged by the Pope when he issued a papal decree granting the Hospitallers protection and privileges. They were supported by gifts from crusaders and from well-meaning donors in Europe, who had an eye on their own salvation paid for by their 'charitable' gifts.

Increasingly, the Hospitallers became involved in the Holy Land war effort – prevention of injuries was as important as curing them. Instead of concentrating on the after-care of the wounded and dying, they sought to protect travellers from attack in the first place by providing an armed escort. This stance evolved so that in the third crusade (1189 - 1192) they played a major military role for the first time. As mentioned earlier, there was rivalry between the Templars and the Hospitallers – the Templars alleging that the Order was created in their image. When the Christians were repulsed from the Holy Land in 1291, both sets of Knights were criticised for their rivalry which it was considered contributed to their defeat - '...divided they fell'.

However, the Hospitallers were not included in the witch-hunt against the Templars and when the latter were dissolved, the majority of the Templar estates were given to the Hospitallers. They provided 'yearly, two chaplains to celebrate divine service in the chapel of the manor' at Temple Dinsley.

Occupiers of Temple Dinsley from 1312

There was a gap between the disbanding of the Templars in 1312 and the granting of Temple Dinsley to the Hospitallers in 1348. R P Mander asserts that in 1307, Temple Dinsley was given to Geoffrey De La Lee probably in settlement of a debt. The Victorian County History states that after 1312, the manor was 'occupied for some years by the lords of the fee' and that it was then let by them to William de Langford for an annual rent of 27 marks. He was still a tenant in 1338.

During this period the Hospitallers became owners of property by virtue of a statute of 1324. As they now had access to the fund-raising activities that were one of the main reasons that the Templars had so much land, in effect the two Orders were merged, despite the fact that the Knights Templar had fallen from grace.

The Hospitallers continued to fight Muslims in the Middle East and the line of battle fronts ebbed and flowed - but the cost of warfare escalated as innovations were introduced - armour was more expensive than chain mail, for example.

From the viewpoint of the villagers at Preston, probably little changed when the Hospitallers became their lords and masters, apart from the personnel at the mansion.

But, although owning Temple Dinsley, the Hospitallers let the estate to a succession of tenants and the holding of religious services became less important.

Preston and the plague of 1349

Preston, indeed the whole of Hertfordshire, felt the virulent grip of the Black Death. It was so severe in Hitchin that everyone died in one district and 'a street became known thereafter as *Dead Street*'.

The BBC documentary, *Christina - a Medieval Woman*, described the remorseless march of the contagion across Hertfordshire. It travelled at a kilometre a day and struck Codicote, which is five miles south-east of Preston, on St Dunstan's Day, 19 May 1349. It would have embraced Preston around this time. Graffiti on a stone pillar of Codicote Church describes the pandemic as 'pitiable, ferocious and violent. Only the dregs of the people are left to bear witness'.

To illustrate the local impact of the plague, Hine, when writing about Stagenhoe (which is a little more than a mile from Preston) said 'the tenants dwindled to a mere handful and the Lord's demesne was left derelict and untilled. The villeins and serfs forsook their manors and with fear of death in their eyes wandered over the country living in woods and hillsides like wild beasts'.

Sixty villages disappeared from the map of Hertfordshire as a result of the Black Death. Preston has its own reminder of this virulent pandemic - Dead Woman's Lane. Local legend has it that the byway was named after the plague victims that were buried at nearby Wayley Close.

Finding the lost manor and hamlet of Welei

But now the sounds of population fail,
No cheerful murmurs fluctuate in the gale,
No busy steps the grass-grown foot-way tread,
For all the bloomy flush of life is fled!

Why are we so fascinated by the lost worlds of the Incas, the Mayas and Atlantis? The historian might reply, it is because of the light they throw on ancient civilisations. Archaeologists would answer that they yearn to examine structures untouched for centuries. But, for most, might it be that they remind us of the fleeting nature of human life – 'we are but a mist, here today, gone tomorrow'?

We don't have to trek thousands of miles to seek out lost civilisations. There are more than 3,000 English deserted villages on our doorstep. Most are no longer 'lost' but 'found', though abandoned.

In Hertfordshire alone, Wikipedia lists 70 deserted villages. Of those, the location of only five remains unknown. These include Welei. Imagine my surprise when I stumbled upon the location of Welei. This is the story of how it happened.

When compiling the history of Preston, a problem arose: in which manor did Preston lie in 1086? While investigating this, my eye was drawn to the manor of Welei which was part of the Royal Manor of Hitchin.

According to the entry in the Domesday Book (above, is a facsimile), Welei was occupied by 8 villeins, 5 bordars, 2 cottars and 4 slaves – and so was probably a settlement of around seventy people – a considerable community by medieval standards. If the slaves lived on the demense farm, then there were likely fifteen homes in the hamlet. Its folk tended 240 acres of arable land, pasture and woodland, where 300 pigs roamed.

But, where exactly was Welei? This question has divided historians. Dr Evelyn Lord suggests that Welei could refer to the local village of Wellhead.

However, Prof. T Williamson writes, '...just to the north of the modern village of Preston lies Wain Wood and the probable site of the lost Domesday vill of Welei'.

Then serendipity played a card. When I research at County Record Offices, I photograph everything, never knowing when an image will prove useful. While looking at a copy of Bryant's map of Hertfordshire dated 1822, I noticed the place-name, Waylay Green *(see below)*. This was near both Preston and Wain Wood. Might Wayley Green be Welei – the names *are* similar?

Then I remembered that I had seen the name Wayley before – this is perhaps a case of when the amateur with an interest in a particular place has an advantage over the trained historian. I re-checked my notes and sure enough the manorial records of Temple Dinsley make several references to the fields of Wayley Wick and Wayley Close.

Not only that, but I also had a newspaper cutting about Preston written by Nina Freebody on file that reported, 'Local legend says that plague victims were buried in Wayley Close only a short distance away from Dead Woman's Lane'.

I had planned a visit to Preston and decided to explore the area around Wayley Green. But where exactly was it? The manorial documents of Temple Dinsley provided the answer. In March 1845, they stated, 'those two closes...called Waley Wick and Waley Close (sic)...(were) afterwards enclosed with.......Woodclose'.

So, the fields Wayley Wick and Waley Close had been absorbed into Woodclose. I pin-pointed Woodclose on the 1818 Enclosure map *(shown on next page)*. The map even noted that 'Wayley Green' lay beside 'Woodclose' and straddled a lane that was known then as Wayley Green Lane and today, as Tatmore Hills Lane.

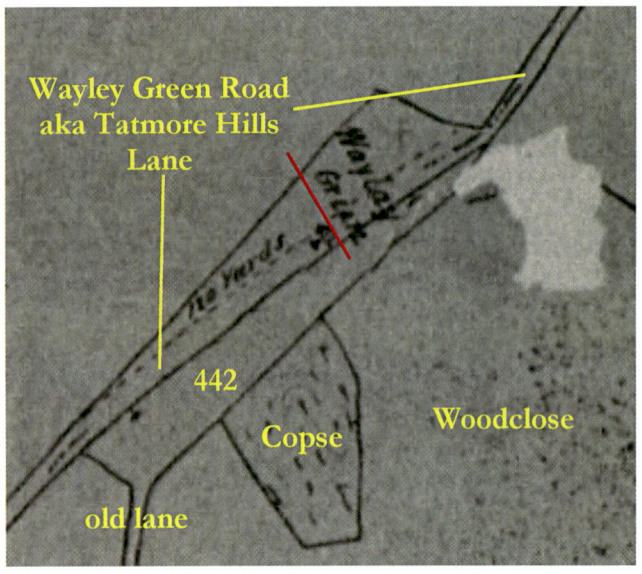

(Above) The copse beside Wayley Green viewed across Woodclose field.

(Above) The 1822 Ippollitts Inclosure Map showing Waylay Green *(sic)* in relation to the lane, copse and Woodclose field. The tract labelled 442 was assigned thus in the enclosure document: 'To William Mellish Esq. a piece of land on Waylay Green with an ancient lane containing one acre, one rood and six perches bounded on the north west by Wayley Green road'.

Sunk are thy bowers in shapeless ruin all,
And the long grass o'ertops the mould'ring wall;
And trembling, shrinking from the spoiler's hand,
Far, far away, thy children leave the land.

So, at 07.30 on 22 April 2010, I stood at the crossroads of Dead Woman's Lane, Tatmore Hills Lane and the Preston to Charlton road *(shown below)*. Encouragingly, what I had taken to be a narrow path to Wayley Green was in fact a wide, sunken track. As I explored the area, I took several photographs.

(Above) Ponds at Wayley Green

The following day, I visited Hertfordshire Record Office (HALS). There, I found a reference which suggested that I might be on the right scent. Preston-born Ian Friel wrote that pagan sites around Hitchin may include, 'Wayley Green (Welei 1086) and Wain Wood. Wayley Green is not to be found on modern maps but it is shown on Bryant's 1822 map of Hertfordshire'. Heartening news, indeed! An academic had spotted the same map reference to Wayley Green and had also associated it with Welei of Domesday!

To summarise what I had established so far: I believed that the 'lost' manor and hamlet of Welei was later known as Wayley Green because:

1) The place names are similar: Welei and Wayley Green.
2) Wayley Green Road is a section of an old byway that leads north from the settlements of St Albans, St Pauls Walden and Stagenhoe to Hitchin. It is also at the intersection of another ancient lane that follows the boundaries of Hitchin and Ippollitts parishes. It is feasible for there to have been a settlement at such a junction.
3) Even today, in the vicinity of Wayley Green there are two ponds and a stream – the life blood of a community.
4) The place-name in 1822 was Wayley *Green*. Where there were Greens, often there were homes.
5) The entry in Domesday for Welei states that there was, *'woodland for 300 pigs'*. Wayley Green today is 300 metres from Wain Wood.

So, why did Welei become deserted? There is a *possible* explanation based on the local legend that plague victims were buried at Wayley Close. The BBC documentary, *Christina – a Medieval Woman* confirmed that plague had struck this district in 1348/49. Did its folk desert Welei because of the effect of plague?

There is some circumstantial evidence that this is what happened. *The Place Names of Hertfordshire* cites several references to Welei until 1342:

> *Just near, since it is always associated in early records with Preston and Dinsley, must have been the D(omesday) B(ook) manor of Welei, Wilei, ...Weyleye 13th Wymondley, 1320, 1342 Ipm, Weylegh, Veyleiedene 14th Hosp, Wyleye juxta Dynesle 1302 Ass.'*

Below is a document (a Grant) which is also dated from the fourteenth century that mentions Weyleye *(sic)*.

Then, allusions to Welei simple peter out. Was this because the Black Death decimated the hamlet?

One archivist has commented, "As for its (Welei's) disappearance, there could have been so many reasons for this; and the Black Death is only one possibility. We are gradually realising that medieval settlement (which in Hertfordshire was not nucleated) was never static. Places grew, declined, and moved all over the landscape, all the time. And I have doubts about the 'plague pit' story. As far as I know Black Death victims would always have been buried in consecrated ground, in the parish churchyard, and 'plague pit' legends usually turn out to be something else - such as the finding of a skeleton which could have been prehistoric, or Roman, or middle Saxon (before churchyard burial became normal). But there was consolidation and retreat from agricultural margins after the Black Death, simply because the population overall had fallen so drastically."

I would only add that given the local legend that victims of plague were buried in Wayley Close and the lack of historical footprints in the area after 1342, I am inclined to the view that the plague of 1348/9 was the main reason for the demise of Welei. I do not see the locals, overtaken by grief and debilitating illness, having the desire or strength to cart the corpses of their people to Ippollitts or Hitchin for interment. Easier by far to bury them nearby and drift off to join other communities.

I felt emboldened to present my research to some local scholars. I was told, "In Preston parish, the 'lost' Domesday vill site of Welei has been positively identified from documentary sources at TL 174260 by Mrs N Freebody. Fieldwork has confirmed this with the finding of late Saxon and 12th century pottery and a medieval roof tile at the site."

So, Preston historian, Nina Freebody *(see page 88)*, had come to the same conclusions! She had even organized a walk-over of the site and registered her findings with the Historic Environmental Record of Herts CC (HER).

There is a clamour of historical references to Welei until 1342. Then, silence. Does this suggest that the hamlet ceased to be because of the Black Death?

Far from being discouraged that Nina had beaten me to the discovery of Welei, I was elated to have it confirmed that I had been on the right track.

Nina often visited Liz Hunter at Preston bursting with news of her latest discoveries. Was her confidante aware of the walkover? I phoned Liz. She not only knew of it, but had participated in it! These are her memories of that day:

"On a crisp, cold, Saturday morning in March 1984, Nina, her husband, Bob, and I visited a field to the north-east of the junction of Tatmore Hills Lane. Nina estimated that the combination of a local small stream rising from a spring, the sloping fields on all sides for grazing livestock and/or for growing crops, and the proximity to the lane (an important cross-country route leading to the thriving early medieval market town of Hitchin), all made this location a possible site for Welei.

"'Field-walking' is a simple, time-consuming but effective technique. It involves traversing the field in a structured way, recording where 'finds' of any artefact have been located. After about an hour of walking, and beginning to feel rather cold, we had found two small fragments of thin, abraded, grey-brown pottery, unglazed and undecorated; each was about one inch square. We were surprised and delighted! On the following Monday, I took the shards to Letchworth Museum where the Keeper of Field Archaeology and a pottery specialist dated them from the 11th/12th century".

Sadly, much of Nina's local history knowledge died with her. While there is a record of her work concerning Welei at HER, it is an irony that information of this 'lost' hamlet has also become lost.

Details of Nina's field work were submitted to the Medieval Village Research Group for their annual report, but owing to an administrative error, they were never actually printed. As a result, English Heritage does not seem to have any files relating to the site of Welei.

I will never forget my sense of history when standing in the middle of this now deserted hamlet. As Robert Sunderland commented, 'It is a strange and somewhat eerie place - much feared when I was young'. Where once there were laughter and tears and the sounds of life and toil, now there is only bird-song. Over the centuries, tumbledown homes have collapsed. The historic byway is now a mere farm track. Two ponds stagnate nearby. Nature has inexorably reclaimed her land - the Green is an tangle of trees and undergrowth. Just beneath the surface of the flora and fauna lie foundations of ancient homes and abandoned artefacts. Skeletons may rest in unmarked graves scattered about the field. Welei is simply no more. It is an evocative spot to take a moment and reflect on the ephemeral nature of human life.

> *Here, as I take my solitary rounds,*
> *Amidst thy tangling walks and ruin'd grounds,*
> *And, many a year elaps'd, return to view*
> *Where once the cottage stood, the hawthorn grew,*
> *Remembrance wakes with all her busy train,*
> *Swells at my breast, and turns the past to pain*

(Quotations from *The Deserted Village* by Oliver Goldsmith)

The manor of Maidencroft is created

There is a link between Edward and Elizabeth de Kendale (whose effigies are in St Mary, Hitchin *(see below)* and the manor of Maidencroft. The manor did not exist at the time of *Domesday* as it was then part of the manor of Dinsley. However, by the middle of the fourteenth century there had been a partition of Dinsley and the new manor of Maidencroft (which was also known as Dinsley Furnival) had been established. Thus, in 1347, it was recorded that when Margaret de Kendale died, she owned 'a tenement (house) called Madecroft *in the manor of Dynsle Furnival*'. Edward was the new Lord of the manor. It follows from this that the size of manors was not set in stone. Indeed, when the local manor of Welei ceased to exist, its land was swallowed by its neighbouring manors, including Temple Dinsley.

Maidencroft manor lay within the parish of Ippollitts, although Salmon noted that it also extended into the parish of Hitchin. In 1427 it was assessed at 287 acres of arable land and 193 acres of pasture. It included fourteen houses, five cottages and a dove house. It included land to the north and east of Preston.

Temple Dinsley from 1350

During the reign of Richard II (1367 - 1400), the Hospitallers continued to reside at Temple Dinsley as the preceptory is mentioned during this period. However, the holding of religious services here appears to have become spasmodic and had probably lapsed by 1498. At this time, the manor was leased (for the duration of his life-time) to John Tong, a preceptor, who undertook to find a chaplain to perform religious services. Two years later Prior Robert Kendal and the Chapter granted a chaplain, Robert Shawe, his board at Dinsley at the table of gentlemen. He was paid five marks to perform services in the chapel.

But, just seven years later, in 1507, the manor was let to Thomas Hobson (and then later to Reginald and Dorothy Adyson) who were also asked to provide the chaplain – the implication being that Shaw was no longer performing this duty. An inventory of the contents of the chapel was taken in 1514. Among the items listed were: a high altar, two smaller altars; images of the Virgin Mary and John the Baptist; three mass books; various vestments; eight altar cloths; a copper cross and a pair of censers. It seems that even if the will to worship was not constant, the accoutrements were available. Another tenant was John Docwa. He asked to be buried at either Temple Dinsley or St Mary, Hitchin.

In 1525, there was a bizarre incident which indicates that Temple Dinsley was moving from its monastic life to a regime of hunting which continued into the twentieth century. 'Henry VIII visited Hitchin and stayed several days there hawking and then went to Temple Dinsley; while following his hawk, in leaping over a ditch with a pole, the pole broke, so that if one, Edmond Moody, a footman, had not leaped into the water and lifted up his head, which was fast in the clay, he would have been drowned.'

The involvement of the Hospitallers at Temple Dinsley ended in 1540 during the dissolution of the monasteries by Henry VIII. They had owned the manor at Preston for almost two centuries. Because of the lapses in providing divine services at Dinsley, apart from the change of ownership, there was probably little change to the daily routine at Dinsley.

Sadleirs at Temple Dinsley (1542 -1712)

Henry VIII evidently was uncaring of the religious privileges of his subjects at Preston – he sold them to one of his principal Secretaries of State and Privy Councillor, Sir Ralph Sadleir (1507 - 1587), together with Temple Chelsin, for £843 2s 6d.

Sadleir was employed in dissolving religious houses such as Temple Dinsley and was wealthy. He was a diplomat who was frequently employed at the Court in Scotland. He was entrusted with Mary Queen of Scots when she was a prisoner at Tutbury Castle. As Sir Ralph had been granted the Manor of Standon, Herts. by Henry VIII, he lived there rather than at Preston. However, his son, Edward Sadleir lived at Temple Dinsley. Following Ralph's death, Temple Dinsley then passed through five members of the Sadleir family over the next 170 years: Sir Ralph; Anne (Sir Ralph's daughter-in-law); Thomas (grandson of Anne); Sir Edwin (son of Thomas) and Sir Edwin jnr.

Thomas Sadleir (a baptist) was at Dinsley during the time of the English Civil War (1642 - 1651). At this time, many in the country were deeply dissatisfied with their monarch, Charles I, and supported the Parliamentarians organised by Oliver Cromwell. After Charles was executed in 1649, England was ruled by a republic until 1660 when control was wrested back by Charles II.

During this period of turbulence, Hitchin (despite its having been a *royal* manor) and its environs were solidly behind the Parliamentarians - it was a Parliamentary stronghold. Thomas Sadleir was an ardent supporter, not least because Sir Ralph Sadlier had been received into the family of Thomas Cromwell. However, one of his younger sons at Temple Dinsley, on the outbreak of war, fled from his father and joined with the Royalist, Prince Rupert.

Hertfordshire saw more of the organisation of the Parliament's armies than any other county in the Eastern Association (which comprised five counties including Hertfordshire) that was formed to raise an army and prevent war from encroaching on their districts. Thomas Sadleir as the grandson of a famous military engineer, Sir Richard Lee, was part of the Council of War for Hertfordshire and served on the Committee of the Eastern Association. Although battles swirled around the Hertfordshire borders, the county saw only a few skirmishes. When the Royalist army led by Rupert threatened Hitchin in 1643, a force of three to four thousand Trained Band Volunteers was mobilised which, in view of Sadleir's involvement, may well have included men from Preston. Several of this force were killed in the fields around Hitchin.

During the winter of 1643/4, the army was billetted at Hitchin, much to the town's peoples' annoyance, and Sadleir was in the party dispatched to Parliament to lobby that their soldiers be removed and that the taxation for their upkeep levied upon Hertfordshire be abandoned. Thomas himself, despite his mansion and 600 acres of land, was no longer able to maintain his son because of these dues.

Cromwell raised another army of 3,000 men from Hitchin, Cambridge and surrounding villages. His recruits came in with 'incredible speed and alacrity' and fought during the Roundhead's victorious battle of Nazeby.

Afterwards, the attention of the Parliamentarians was drawn to Ireland where Sadleir served as Adjutant-General with some of his Hitchin soldiers. He stormed Ballydoyne, Graney, Dunhill and Clonmell and was made Governor of Galway.

Present-day Preston may retain a memorial of these times. Hine wrote that, in 1691, the village green at Preston was known as Cromwell's Green. The source of this information is unknown, but possibly Hine may have been referring to what is known today as Crunnells Green - an area in the village adjacent to the grounds of Temple Dinsley. In 1713, it was called 'Cranwells Green'.

Meanwhile, at Temple Dinsley after 1540, without the patronage of the nuns of Elstree, the chapel at Preston soon fell into decay and ruin. By 1700, it was reported that, 'no trace of this building now remains'. In the first few years of the eighteenth century, Sir Edwin Sadleir was forced to sell Temple Dinsley and its land which included the *Offley Holes Farm* to offset his crippling debts.

Minsden Chapel and the rebellion of Preston villagers

A study of Minsden Chapel c.1840

During the Reformation (from 1538) worship at Minsden chapel declined. The congregation was small and couldn't afford a minister. As the local people were too independent to travel to St Mary's Church at Hitchin, every few months a clergyman rode to Minsden to conduct baptism, marriage and burial services. The chapel continued to drift apart from its mother and became increasingly neglected.

In 1650, a report noted 'that no dues had been paid to the Vicar of Hitchin for many years (by Minsden); that it had been destitute of a preaching minister for divers years past; that the chapel had fallen into great decay'. Then, incredibly, it added that 'it was fit to be made a parish church'. However, their hopes were dashed. Although a considerable amount of money was raised for repairs (and a new roof was built) the custodians of the fund died and the money was lost. No aid was forthcoming for these poor from St Nicholas! This reversal was quickly followed by a shattering decision.

Although the villagers had never paid a church rate to St Mary at Hitchin and their own chapel was in desperate need of refurbishment, it was decreed that they should pay a rate for repairs to the church *at Hitchin*. To enforce this order, in 1688, twenty-four actions were brought against the folk of Preston and Langley. The list of Preston's inhabitants who were liable to pay the rate reads like a 'Who's Who' of the village at the end of the seventeenth century and the rate levied allows a comparison of the extent of their property.

....our chapel "is now totally ruinated, stripped, uncovered, decayed and demolished"

The two leaders of the villagers, John Holton and John Farr, were excommunicated and imprisoned because they refused to obey the decision. In the face of overwhelming power and influence, the people of Preston and Langley bowed to the inevitable and paid their dues under protest. Two years later, in 1690, they sent a report to the archdeacon that their chapel 'is now totally ruinated, stripped, uncovered, decayed and demolished' – the underlying, accusing message was that this was the direct consequence of St Mary's actions.

Now Minsden chapel began to be plundered. Jeremiah Godfrey stole 400 pounds of lead in 1690. Stone and oak fittings from the chapel were carted to cottages for *their* repair and decoration. In 1700 Joseph Arnold of Langley was sued by John Heath, the chapel warden of Minsden who lived at Preston Green, for appropriating the font for a sink at his home. Painted glass from the chapel was found at *The Sun* inn at Hitchin and it was alleged that in 1840, when the church at Ippollitts was restored, the tracery work of the windows was stolen from Minsden.

About this time, a Hitchin character known as 'old Bowstock' would load his donkey cart with 'clunch' or rubble at Minsden and travel to Hitchin market where he then sold it ironically in the shadow of St Mary.

Even the three bells of Minsden chapel were looted. In 1725, a probable witness to the removal of two of them, John Reason of St Pauls Walden, was returning home from Hitchin market and was near Hitch Wood when he was alarmed by the noise of men with horses and a fast-moving carriage. They were travelling towards Harpenden. Shortly afterwards, the bells were reported as missing. It was said by Mr Cook of Little Almshoe that one of his barns was called 'Bell Barn' as the third stolen bell had been hidden there one night.

Much of this pillage occurred when the chapel was still being used as a place of worship. The chapel warden, John Heath, was admonished because of his leanings towards the Baptists and Independents.

Heath allowed an Independent Christian, Daniel Skingle, to use the chapel to preach to his flock. The congregation quickly swelled to around 300 souls, but Skingle and Heath were rebuked by the Church and were forced to make an abject confession of offences against God and the Church.

Skingle's sermons were the last to be preached at Minsden, but marriages continued to be performed there. Despite its being a ruined shell, there was a certain appeal in its rustic surroundings. It was hidden among trees and adorned with moss and ivy. Cooing doves witnessed the wedding ceremonies and the view of elms through the holes in the roof heightened the rural atmosphere. The chapel also had the allure of a hint of superstition. The further it fell into rack and ruin, the more couples wanted to marry there. Instead of being entered in the chapel register at Minsden, these later marriages were recorded in the parish register of St Mary. On 11 July 1738/9, the baker, Enoch West married Mary Horn at the chapel. Beside their names 'at Minsden chapel' was written for the last time. During the ceremony it was reported that a lump of masonry fell and dashed the service book from the curate's hand. After this narrow escape, the Bishop of Lincoln would not allow any other marriages at Minsden – a wedding could become a wake.

'Is this the place where numerous footsteps trod,
Where living votaries filled the House of God ;
Where the full chorus of the sounding choir
Bid one loud strain of prayer and praise aspire?
How silent now the desolated spot,
Its paths untrodden and its use forgot.
Of noxious reptiles now the haunted scene,
Hung with cold dews, and clad with baleful green
All day the redbreast mournful ditty sings;
With mournful ditties, plaintive echo rings;
And birds ill-omened at the day's decline
With boding sounds profane the hallowed shrine;
While mournful shadows stretched along the plains
Move with the wind and scare benighted swains.'

'On the Ruins of Minsden Chapel' by Wallis

Minsden Chapel in recent times

Minsden Chapel slowly but inexorably succumbed to man and nature. In 1907, the Hitchin photographer, TW Latchmore took some photos at the Chapel. He saw nothing unusual while there but asserted that when he was 'back in my studio developing the plates...I noticed this strange image on one of them. I do not claim it is a ghost. It may only be due to some freak of light and shade, but it is extraordinary, is it not?'

Latchmore related this story and showed his photograph *(right)* of the mysterious monk to Elliott O'Donnell, a writer of the occult. Intrigued, O'Donnell collected a party together to visit Minsden on Halloween Night, 1923. He was accompanied by three journalists, a schoolmaster, a lady with reputed psychic powers and Latchmore. O'Donnell wrote, 'We arrived at Minsden Wood shortly before midnight'. The reporters refused to separate, 'they were all huddled together under one of the arches, waiting with bated breath for whatever might happen'. The psychic donned a witches costume and sat down chanting dismally. Nothing came, however, and we were all beginning to despair of any phenomenon when suddenly one of our number with a loud ejaculation, pointed to a white light shimmering though the naked branches of a tree..."It's come at last", someone whispered....and we saw what looked like a figure clad in the white costume of a nun standing in front of the arches....to our intense disappointment...(it proved to be) a curious and distinctly eerie effect of moonbeams and shadow'. When the group left at 0400, they agreed that 'if it was not haunted, it *ought* to be, for a more eerie spot none of us had ever been in'.

Five years later, Latchmore confessed. He said that he had been conducting a carefully planned experiment when the original photograph was taken. A friend (Reginald Hine?) was draped in a hooded sheet and lurked before the ruins as a timed exposure was taken. The camera shutter was then closed, the 'ghost' moved away and the exposure was completed – which produced the final photo. Reginald Hine, now the lessee of Minsden Chapel, published the photograph and effectively preserved the sense of mystery that surrounded his property.

Hine wrote, 'Minsden is for those whose minds are in ruins; for those sons of quietness who are distracted by the crimes and follies and misfortunes of mankind. In its deep shade, many who have been brought low by the cares of this world, or in my case by the wear and tear of my profession, have found healing, consolation and repose....the very air at Minsden is tremulous with that faint susurrus – call it the under-song of the earth, the music of the spheres, the sigh of departed time or what you will – which only the more finely attuned spirits overhear'.

And so the hocus-pocus hokum that enshrouds Minsden is perpetuated. The internet is agog with stories and rumours and 'feelings' that centre on the site. But today, it is protected by Hine. He warned off trespassers and scavengers, threatening pursuit with 'the utmost vigour of the law'. He wished to be buried there and promised that he would 'endeavour in all ghostly ways to protect and haunt its hallowed walls'. The first part of his wish was granted in part at least as his ashes were scattered at the Chapel's entrance.

(Above) In 2010, one chapel wall (in the foreground) has crumbled to the ground and the rest are unstable

For my part, I must confess that when I visited Minsden, I experienced a tingling feeling of the urtica dioica variety. As I type these notes, my eye is drawn to the flint from the Chapel that has pride of place on my desk. When the moon is full, my study is lit by sparks, there is a 'whoosh' and a whiff of steam and sulphur. I'm not convinced that they emanate from my computer's hard-drive.

John Bunyan and Preston

Wain Wood, to the north of Preston, will always be linked with John Bunyan (1628-1688) - the Bedfordshire Baptist preacher who wrote *Pilgrim's Progress*. Reginald Hine described this association in this way:

> *'At Wain Wood, in Hitchin parish, there was no preaching shed. The cottage is still there with its pleasant ingle-nook in which Bunyan smoked many a peaceful pipe. But it was in the woodland dell which is still known as Bunyan's Dell, under the trees and under the stars, that he preached to his "gathered church" which numbered sometimes over a thousand souls. If it drenched with rain, there were four devoted women ever at hand to hold an apron over his bare head as he preached.'*

One of Bunyan's circuitous preaching tours was by way of Harlington, Bendish, Wain Wood, Meldreth, Gamlingay and so back to Bedford. Hitchin people would steal away to met him at Bendish or at Wain Wood, usually at dead of night. The chief anxiety in this district was the threat of discovery and scouts were posted on Tatmore Hills to give a warning of the approach of officers of the law from Hitchin.

John Brown in his biography, *John Bunyan (1885)*, described the tradition of Bunyan's visits to Preston (between 1872 and 1875) as being 'stronger still': 'About three miles from (Hitchin) stood in those days the country house known as Hunsdon House, and afterwards as Preston Castle.....(at) Wain Wood there was a green space, forming a sort of ampitheatre which has come to be called, Bunyan's Dell *(shown below)*. It is capable of holding several hundred people and here while the loneliness of the wood sheltered them from their enemies and friendly scouts kept watch on every side, Bunyan often preached.'

'There were those living near who were in earnest sympathy with him: the Widow Heath at Preston was licensed for a Congregational meeting place on 2 May 1672 and a licence was granted to Thomas Milway to be congregational teacher there.' Brown also refers to the Foster brothers of Hunsdon House who bore 'honoured names in the annals of Nonconformity'. Their house 'was an asylum of the persecuted....there was no guest more frequent or more welcome at their fireside than Bunyan himself'.

(Above) The Wain Wood cottage where Bunyan stayed and its inglenook fireplace

A view of Temple Dinsley c. 1700

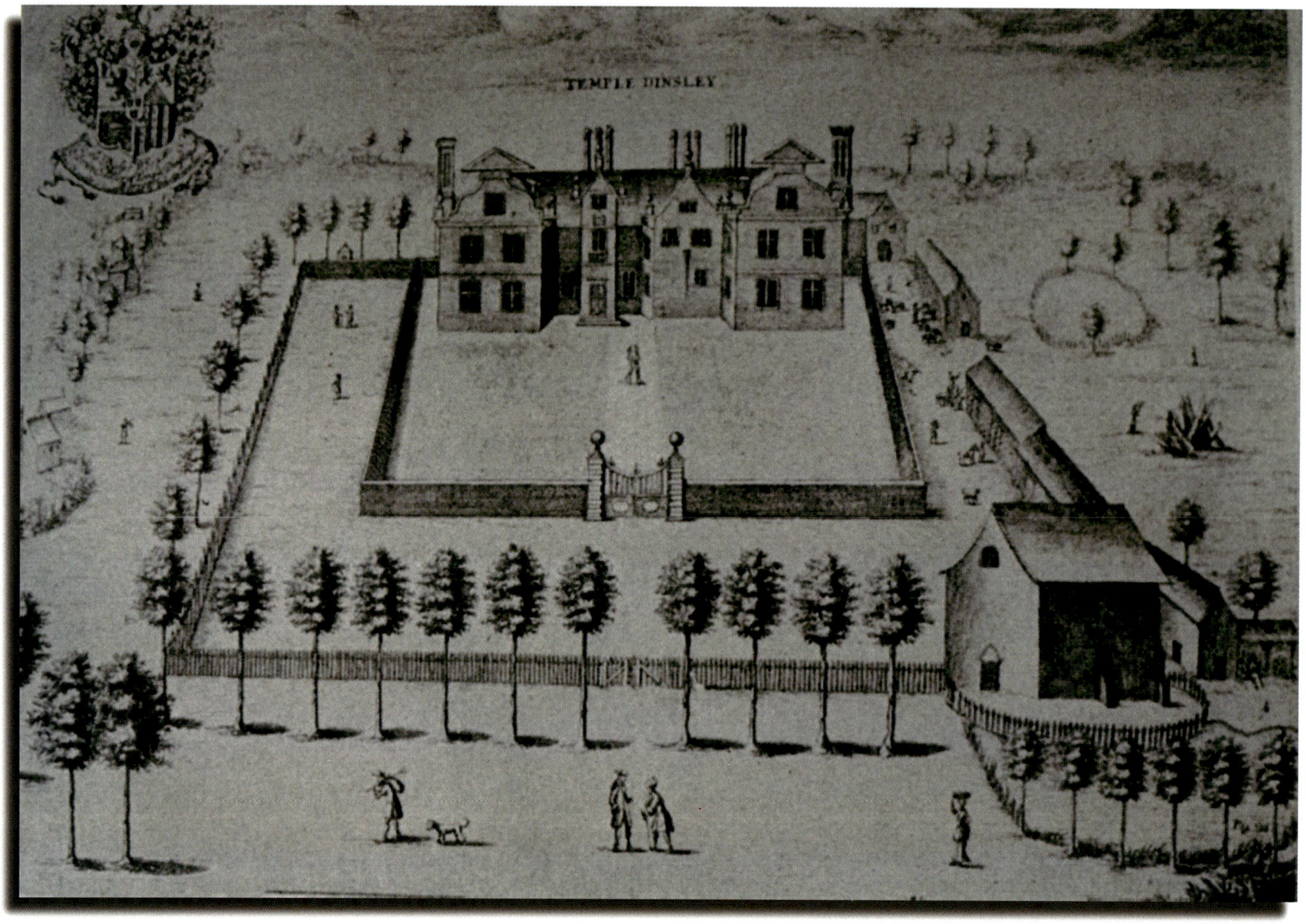

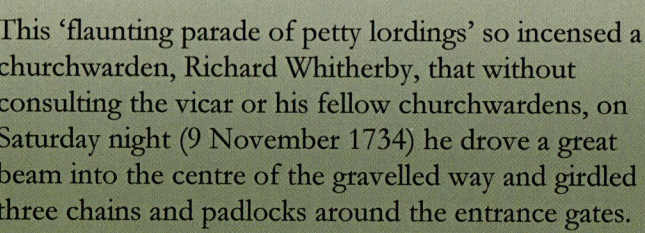

The houses of Preston seem to be shown to the right together with a collection of buildings which probably include stables. It is likely that a mill is also shown here in the right foreground - the edifice has a medieval hood-mould that may date from the thirteenth century.

Benedict Ithell buys Temple Dinsley

Benedict Ithell was the deputy treasurer of Chelsea Hospital. In August 1712, he bought Temple Dinsley for £3,922. Possibly Ithell purchased the estate for the hunting potential of the land around the building rather than the house itself. The Sadleirs were not able to maintain the house in a good state of repair because two years later, in 1714, Ithell demolished Dinsley and built a new mansion close-by. The house had a heraldic badge of a rising bird and the inscription '1714' on rainwater heads. According to archaeological findings and radar surveys in 2000, the mansion was just to the east of the old building which was sited under the present-day rose garden. He also restored estate cottages in Preston.

Ithell *(above)* was appointed as Sheriff of Hertfordshire in 1727 and was also made a trustee of Hitchin Grammar School. He formed a bond with Ralph Radcliffe of Hitchin Priory.

The pair drove to St Mary's Church at Hitchin on Sundays in a style guaranteed to upset the church wardens. Their gilded coaches were 'emblazoned with arms and their crests glittering in silver radiance from every part of the harness where a crest could possibly be placed'. They swung through the south gates and along the gravelled path of the graveyard to the entrance of the porch to the accompaniment of the tolling church bells. The pageant was 'brought up in style with straining and struggling of horses, cracking of whip, glistening of harness and flashing of wheels through gravel, horses fretted into a foam, dashing the pebbles against the poor pedestrian people'.

This 'flaunting parade of petty lordings' so incensed a churchwarden, Richard Whitherby, that without consulting the vicar or his fellow churchwardens, on Saturday night (9 November 1734) he drove a great beam into the centre of the gravelled way and girdled three chains and padlocks around the entrance gates.

He reckoned without the resourcefulness of Radcliffe. He sent his carpenter to break the chains and saw down the offending beam - all this just in time for Ithell to drive through in triumph. Whitherby still had some cards to play. On the Monday morning, he summonsed both the carpenter, for malicious damage, and Ithell's coachman, for trespass. They escaped on the grounds that no apparent annoyance had been visited on the corpses in the graveyard! While this makes for a good story, if this was typical of the man, one wonders how such a squire behaved towards the 'poor people' of Preston.

Benedict Ithell snr (67) died on 8 July 1737. He was interred within St Mary's Church immediately below a magnificent monument. His son, Benedict jnr, was also buried at St Mary and a reader featuring him is on a wall *(right)*. Benedict snr's will was proved on 14 September 1737. He asked to be buried 'in the vault lately made by me in the parish church of Hitchin'. He left to each of his daughters, Elizabeth, Mary and Martha a legacy of £2,000. His estate was left to his son, Benedict jnr and thence, if he died without issue, to his daughters. They all later died without marrying and were buried at St Mary, Hitchin. In her will of 3 April 1767, Martha Ithell bequeathed the estate of Temple Dinsley to Thomas Harwood, her 'faithful friend and steward'.

The reading of her will caused uproar. Her cousin, Benedict Clarke of London claimed in Chancery that Martha was of unsound mind – but lost his case. Thomas Harwood was installed as the new Lord of Dinsley Manor.

Thos. Harwood inherits Temple Dinsley

Thomas Harwood's remarkable social elevation is well mirrored in the Hitchin Militia Lists. From 1758 he was described as 'servant', 'gentleman's servant' and even 'labourer'. Then, in 1768, he is Thomas Harwood, 'Esquire'! But tongues were wagging in the village. Why had Thomas received this valuable windfall?

When Thomas in turn left his estate to Joseph Darton, even in the twentieth century, a newspaper reported, 'some suggested that Joseph Darton was his son by a secret marriage to Martha Ithell or that he was a nephew or cousin'. Even today the Preston Village web site states that Joseph Darton was the 'secret son' of Martha and Thomas.

> *A newspaper reported, "some suggested that Joseph Darton was (Harwood's) son by a secret marriage to Martha Ithell or that he was a nephew or cousin".*

I have not seen any documents which support this claim. It may be true or it may be tittle-tattle that has been handed down in the village. However, there is some evidence that refutes these rumours - Thomas may well have had a nephew named 'Darton'. This information emerges from details in his will.

Thomas Harwood's will was drawn up on 10 January 1786. He left annuities to his brother John Harwood (£100) and his sister, Ursula *Darton* (£50). He bequeathed his manor and property in Hertfordshire to his 'nephew, Joseph Darton'. Legacies were left as follows: nephew, Thomas Harwood - £100; the other children of brother John Harwood - £30 each; niece, Sarah Kitchener ('wife of Benjamin' - Benjamin Kitchener married Sarah *Darton* at Knebworth, Herts. on 19 January 1782) - £400; friend, Edward Kitchener (a farmer at Preston) - £100; Robert Heathcore - £20; his servants at the time of his death - £10 each 'for mourning. The residue of his estate was given to Joseph Darton.

So, wonderful details of Thomas' immediate family are provided by his will. He had a brother, John (who was a mere servant at Great Wymondley with a lame/sore leg). He also had a sister, Ursula (who married Michael Darton at Shephall, Hertfordshire on 16 May 1749. The couple had at least one child, Sarah). Thomas' origins can also be confirmed from this information. As he was born on 17 January 1725 at Bennington, Herts., the son of John and Sarah Harwood. Thomas was therefore 62 years old when he died.

Two undeniable facts are apparent. Firstly, Thomas showed generosity towards several nephews and nieces in his will. Secondly, it was possible that he did indeed have a nephew with the surname, 'Darton' towards whom he also showed extreme favour - he certainly had a niece named, 'Darton'. But, I would be happier if the baptism of Joseph Darton could be found in parish registers - but there again, Sarah Darton's baptism also cannot be located.

There is a further indication that Joseph Darton's father was Michael. When Joseph baptised his children, evidently following a naming pattern, he had his fourth son christened Michael - a relatively unusual name at the time.

A possible explanation for the absence of Joseph and Sarah Darton's baptism is that perhaps there was a Quaker influence in the family. Joseph Darton's wife, Elizabeth, was a Quaker. This means that they may not be have been married in an Anglican church. On balance, from the facts outlined above, possibly Joseph Darton was indeed Thomas Harwood's nephew.

There is one further curious detail: the Court Baron for Maidencroft recorded in 1787 that John Harwood of Great Wymondley was Thomas' 'only brother *and heir*'. John promptly surrendered Thomas' property to Joseph Darton.

Robert Hinde at Preston Castle

Robert Hinde *(shown above)* was born at Chertsey Abbey, Surrey in 1720/1. On his paternal side, his ancestors included Scottish and English kings as far back as Alfred the Great.

The line of his maternal family reputedly could be traced to the Emperor Charlemagne. Another of his kin was an attendant of William the Conqueror.

Robert's family, although steeped in military tradition, had purchased a brewery at Holborn, London, to bolster finances. From the profits of this venture, Robert's father bought Hunsdon House at Preston. This mansion had been built on the site of Preston Castle which dated from around the tenth century. It was rumoured that a battle had been fought in the area 'in early times' and that one of the protagonists had been based at Preston Castle.

Unsurprisingly, in view of his military forefathers, Robert joined the army in 1751 and was appointed as Ensign in the Eleventh Foot. Three years later, he was promoted to the rank of Sub-Brigadier and Cornet in the Second Horse Guards. During a lull in campaigns, Robert married Mary Ball who was the daughter of the Governor of Jersey. The couple had seventeen children.

After his parents' deaths in the early 1750s, Robert inherited Hunsdon House and embarked on a programme of bizarre additions to the property *(shown below - a sketch by Samuel Lucas)*.

He converted the appearance of the house into that of a castle (from which it derives its later name, Preston Castle) by making turrets, embattlements, port holes, port cullises and so on. He raised a small battery of seven guns on the right hand-side of the entrance to the House and planted a larger gun in front of the same, all of which were fired on particular rejoicing days.

Robert also erected a building, which he called a gazebo, in one of his fields called 'Mount Garrison'. 'In the garden adjoining he raised his earthworks, dug his trenches and built his mimic fortifications'.

If these modifications were insufficient to raise the eyebrows of Preston's labourers, Robert also began behaving eccentrically – 'On anniversaries of the King's birthday and of famous battles, he mounted his servant, Samuel Pilgrim, on horseback and made him ride through Hitchin trumpeting as he went and stopping occasionally to proclaim, like a herald of old, the event for which the day was famous'. This odd behaviour escalated. Robert later dressed in full uniform and decorations and rode to Hitchin's market place with his retainers to announce important dates in English heritage. There was a fanfare, an address and the national anthem was sung, after which entertainment the entourage beat a retreat to Preston Castle.

After playing soldiers, in 1756 Robert was no doubt delighted to experience the real McCoy when he fought in the Seven Years War in the Light Cavalry. He was again promoted and finished the campaign as *Captain* Hinde. Intrigued (perhaps obsessed) as he was with the tactics of war, after his retirement in 1763 Robert wrote, *The Discipline of the Light Horse* which was a history of his regiment.

Robert returned to Preston Castle on half-pay. But his make-believe soldiering continued. His 'army' included his swelling progeny and the eight children of Mary Taylor who lived at Hitchin Hill. These were decked-out in scarlet uniforms, blue sash and black beaver hat and called Robert, 'General'.

He now applied himself to farming – yet his military training asserted itself even in this pursuit. When he summoned and dismissed his labourers, it was proclaimed by a chorus from his Light-Horse bugle. However, he took his farming seriously – 'I pursue the following method: wheat after the fallow, then peas, turnips, barley, oats, clover, wheat'. He suggested improvements to Arthur Young's swing-plough and trialled the Hertfordshire great-wheel plough and the one-handle Essex plough.

He found time to sit on the Hitchin Bench and also lambasted the surveyors of highways over the state of local roads. His attention to detail and egotism drove him to correct an entry of the birth of one of his children in the Hitchin parish register.

Robert added 'Esquire' to the record and noted his rank and regiment. It must have been galling to find that half-pay did not adequately cover his expenses - and especially the demands of his children. He sometimes rode to London in an attempt to have the £132.0s.5½d paid early.

It was on St George's Day (ironically the day that his pay was due), 23 April 1786, that Robert (66) died. On the day of the funeral, Pilgrim fired a salute and sounded the 'Last Post' from the gazebo. Then, the last Hinde military procession, resplendent in its heraldry and plumes, wound its way through the Preston lanes to St Mary's Church at Hitchin.

> *"And how can you imagine such a character as my Uncle Toby(Shandy)?"*
> *"It was drawn from life. It is a portrait of....Captain Hinde"*

Robert was laid to rest with his parents inside St Mary, but even here he attracted attention – the churchwardens objected to the verse on his grave and his Coat of Arms was prone to trip worshippers. The verse and indentation have now been eroded.

Five Generations of Dartons at Temple Dinsley

Joseph Darton (? - 1795)
Joseph Darton (1776 - 1816) married Elizabeth Wilson who died in 1852.
Thomas Harwood Darton (1811 - 1858)
Thomas Harwood Darton (1848 - 1887)
Thomas Harwood Darton (1880 - 1969)

The first five people noted, including Elizabeth, were Lords of the Manor of Temple Dinsley.

Joseph Darton (? - 1795)

There is evidence that Joseph did not reside during all this period at Temple Dinsley, thus setting a pattern for his descendents. In 1794, the Austrian composer, Joseph Hayden (1732 - 1809), was taken to Preston by his friend the 4th Earl of Abingdon, a music patron, to visit the 6th Baronet Aston (of Cheshire) and his wife Jane. While there, Hayden wrote some music that may have included a song sung by himself and the two nobleman. This took place at Temple Dinsley, the inference being that the Darton's were living elsewhere.

The following year, 1795, Joseph Darton was dead. The copy of his will is somewhat difficult to read, but he appears to leave an annuity of £200 to his wife Elizabeth and legacies of £1,000 to his children, Thomas, Edmund, Michael and Betty.

The residue of Joseph snr's estate was left to his son, Joseph Darton. Elizabeth was to be allowed to remain at Temple Dinsley. Joseph's executors were Edward Kitchener (a Preston farmer) and Edward Evans who were given £100 each 'for their trouble'.

On 28 January 1799, there was a development in the religious life of Joseph's widow, Elizabeth. She was a Quaker, having been recommended to the Hitchin meeting by their brethren at Westminster. But Elizabeth had become 'very slack in attendance' and 'despite caution and counsel' which had not produced 'the desired effect' and as she did not show 'a disposition to change' she was disowned from the faith. The decision was recorded by William Lucas jnr.

Joseph Darton, jnr (1795 - 1816)

Joseph was eighteen when he inherited Temple Dinsley and his tenure lasted a mere twenty-one years - he was forty when he died. In his will (dated 16 June 1807 and witnessed by Robert Harwood, John Young and Samuel Peete, constable) Joseph expressed his wish to be buried in the family vault at St Mary's Church, Hitchin, where his father already lay. A memorial was erected to him therein.

Joseph's property in Bedfordshire, Hertfordshire and Middlesex was left to his widow, Elizabeth, who was also bequeathed Joseph's personal property. Each of their children who survived to the age of twenty-one was to receive £100 annually, paid in four instalments.

After Elizabeth died, her trustees (Edward Cobb, supervisor of excise, and John Marshall, liquor merchant, both of Hitchin) were to distribute the rents and profits after debts had been paid in equal amounts to Joseph's surviving children who also inherited his estate in equal shares. However, as Thomas Harwood Darton was the only child to survive Elizabeth's death, he was in effect Joseph's sole heir.

Elizabeth Darton (1816 - 1852)

Soon after Joseph's death (and probably in 1818), perhaps due to economic necessity or simply because the mansion was too big, Elizabeth let Temple Dinsley to the Hitchin brewer, Henry Crabbe (born 1796). Henry and Fanny Crabbe (nee Ellis) had seven children, at least six of whom were born when the family were at Temple Dinsley. Fanny was the daughter of Thomas Flower Ellis who owned land around Preston.

Henry had acquired malt houses at Bull Corner, Hitchin and four fields in Ippollitts. He was also in partnership with Joseph Margotts Pierson (brewer) of a property at Cock Street, Hitchin and with John Marshall (brewer) of a house and brew-house at Sun Street, Hitchin.

However, Henry died on 19 June 1830 and the process of trying to let Temple Dinsley began again. In May 1832, the house was advertised in *The Times*. It was described as a family mansion in an elevated and airy situation, delightfully sheltered by timber. On the ground floor was a breakfast parlour, dining and drawing room, gentleman's dressing room with adjoining bathroom. On the first floor were three large bedrooms, each of which had its own dressing room. There were six large attics.

In the grounds there were two double coach-houses, stabling for seven horses (above which were four servants' rooms) and large walled gardens. Near the stables was a large brick dovecote. *Temple Farm* with its 234 acres was also available to let, either with the mansion or separately.

The additional appeal of the rights to shooting on the Temple Dinsley manor's 200 acres of woodland was highlighted. It was about this time (1832) that the two views of Temple Dinsley *(that follow)* were drawn. The stables and dovecote can be seen clearly.

A year later and, as no tenant for the mansion had been found, with a hint of desperation more advertisements appeared in May 1833: 'To be let and entered upon immediately'. This time, the hunting aspect of the area was highlighted as the property was 'near the Sebright hounds, the meets of Lord Petre's hounds and only three miles from the harriers of F P Delme-Radcliffe'.

Temple Dinsley was unoccupied in 1837 but had been let probably by mid-1839 to newly-weds Thomas (bn 1815) and Frederica Halsey. In 1840 the Halseys spent an incredible £1800 (after discount!) to bring the fittings and furnishing of the house up to their standards. There is an itemised record of thirty-six pages of this refurbishment, the cost of which was equal to the total annual wages of sixty farm labourers. However, the Halseys did not stay long and had probably moved out in the mid-1840s. On 24 May 1844, a son was born at Temple Dinsley who lived but a few hours. In 1846, Thomas was a Member of Parliament and eight years later, Thomas, Frederica and another son drowned when the steamer, *Ercolano*, foundered in the Gulf of Genoa.

In 1841, Elizabeth Darton was living at *Bunyan's Cottage* in Wain Wood and her son, Thomas Darton, and his young wife were at Offley. Ten years later, Thomas and Maria Darton and their five young children were back at Temple Dinsley and Elizabeth was living either at *The Cottage* or *Bunyan's Cottage*.

Elizabeth died in 1852. There was a touching news report of her funeral: 'On Thursday, 18 November 1852, the mortal remains of Mrs Darton were deposited in the family vault in Hitchin Church.

'They were bourne to the tomb and followed thither by the tenantry of the Temple Dinsley estate, most of whom, with their fathers before them had for many generations lived and laboured on the property. In her, the poor have really lost a friend, for while her attention was more especially directed to the wants and needs of her poorer neighbours, still the houseless wanderer never sought relief from her in vain.' There is circumstantial evidence that Elizabeth was instrumental in the building of the first school at Preston, as we will see.

Now, Thomas Harwood Darton snr was Lord of the Manor. He held this position for just five years until his death on 12 February 1858. Almost immediately, Temple Dinsley was advertised to be let on 11 May 1858. But, in 1861, Thomas' widow, Maria, was still in residence there.

By 1871, retired builder John Weeks and his wife, Lucy were living in the mansion and Thomas and Maria were at *The Cottage*. Weeks was a fellow of the Royal Horticultural Society who designed and built horticultural buildings, such as large, ornate greenhouses that were heated by hot water. He exhibited at the Great Exhibition of 1851. Weeks died at Temple Dinsley on 13 August 1879.

Clearly the Dartons could not afford to keep the estate so in 1873, the entire estate was advertised, not to be let, but to be sold. The sale particulars provided a wonderful description of the estate and its various parts. Illustrating the way in which Temple Dinsley dominated Preston is the statement that for sale was 'nearly the entire village...about forty cottages and *The Chequers* public house'.

PRELIMINARY NOTICE OF AN IMPORTANT SALE

THE TEMPLE DINSLEY ESTATE,

The Temple Dinsley estate included three farms:
- Temple Farm
- Poynders End Farm (90 acres)
- Austage End Farm (41 acres)

The house was described as a 'fine, old mansion'. It had a spacious hall, drawing room, billiard room, dining room, morning room, study and gun room on the ground floor - all of which were centrally heated (in 1873!). On the next floor were seven bedrooms, three dressing rooms, a bathroom and two toilets. The roof space had six attics.

When the sale of Temple Dinsley was advertised, its agricultural potential was not promoted. The selling point was the opportunity for field sports such as the hunting and shooting of foxes, pheasants, partridges, rabbits and hares. 'It is in a favourite hunting district....the sporting capabilities are of a high character and afford excellent partridge and pheasant shooting'. This emphasis on hunting explains in part why the woods around Preston survived. While there was some revenue from the sale of rights to coppice trees, the woods were mainly preserved as the haunt of wild-life which could be hunted.

The Pryors at Temple Dinsley (1873)

Temple Dinsley was sold to Major Henry Pryor of Clifton House, near Biggleswade, Beds. His sons, Ralston de Vins and Geoffrey Pryor were later involved in the running of the estate and collecting rents. The Pryors were 'old Hertfordshire stock' being brewers and maltsters and Henry was a retired soldier. He had recently received bequests and legacies from relatives and bought a large portion of the estate of the estate clearly intending that his two young sons would manage it when they grew older. He paid £19,000, and a further £1,902 was added to the price for timber rights. This outlay was possibly a stretch for Henry as he arranged to pay £9000 and raised a mortgage for the residue.

It is worth noting that according to the 1871 census, Major Pryor's household at Clifton included a visitor, William H Darton. Henry Pryor and William were serving as Captain and Lieutenant in the 7th Bedfordshire regiment. Two years later, Henry had purchased Temple Dinsley from William's brother, Captain Thomas Darton. In 1881, Thomas Darton was renting *The Cottage* from the Pryors.

Although the Pryors now owned the estate, they didn't live at Temple Dinsley. Within months of Weeks' death, the pattern of letting the mansion was repeated when once again, on 6 December 1879, the remaining lease of eleven years was advertised as being available. Several thousand pounds had recently been spent on the property.

The new residents in 1881 were Henry Brand (39) *(shown right)*, his wife, Susan, and their five children. He was a magistrate and a Liberal Member of Parliament, serving as Speaker in the House of Commons between 1872 and 1884. Following the death of his father, he became Lord Hampden. Brand served as governor of New South Wales, Australia and is the greatx2 grandfather of Sarah Ferguson, the Duchess of York.

Bunyan's Chapel, Church Lane

The mother church of Preston's Chapel was the Tilehouse Street Baptist Church (Salem) at Hitchin. In view of Preston's place in the Bunyan tradition and also the strength of feeling for the faith in the village - in 1886, about half of the villagers claimed to be Baptist - a chapel was built to the north of Preston Green. The project cost £450, of which £100 was paid for the garden in which it was erected.

The foundation stones were laid on Thursday, 5 April 1877 by Edward and Ebenezer Foster of Cambridge who were descendants of the Foster brothers of *Castle Farm*.

The Chapel was well supported in its early days. In February 1882 there was a tea meeting on a Wednesday evening at the chapel which attracted 150 villagers and friends. The chapel's Sunday School had eight teachers and 70 scholars. The momentum of encouraging attendances at the chapel was maintained. At the anniversary services in June of 1882, so many were in attendance (300) that the evening service was held on The Green. The collection and proceeds from the tea raised £11 and it was noted that the Sunday School now had 12 teachers and 90 students.

Religious apathy and the cost of building repairs ('the floor was a bit dicey') resulted in the closure of the chapel in 1987. By then there were just four or five faithful souls in the congregation and the Sunday School had also declined although eleven attenders were from one family, the Browns.

The closing service was held on Sunday, 9 August 1987. Ministers and friends from Tilehouse Street and Wymondley attended the service including Mollie Foster who maintained the link with the Foster family of the seventeenth century. *Bunyan's Chapel* had been used as a place of worship in Preston for a century. *(Below, the chapel's interior.)*

Fire at Temple Dinsley (1888)

The Temple Clock regulated the lives of the villagers *(see page 83)*. The clock was destroyed by fire in May, 1888. This, from the Hertfordshire Mercury:

> *FIRE. Early on Wednesday morning the brigade was called to a fire at Temple Dinsley, the residence of the Hon. H. Brand. On their arrival they found the coachman's residence, stabling, coach house, fowl house and other extensive outbuildings, one mass of fire. The brigade quickly set to work with their steam machine to prevent the fire extending to the house, which they succeeded in doing. It appeared there had been a fire in the chimney of the building the previous afternoon and it is supposed this was the cause of the outbreak. Six horses were saved but the fire spread with so much rapidity that it was impossible to save anything else. The furniture in the coachman's house was all destroyed with a large quantity of hay, straw, harness, a stack of hay and several carts.*

By 1891, the lease of Temple Dinsley had expired and the mansion was unoccupied, although probably the Brands had left earlier - the last of Mrs Brand's visits to Preston School was on 13 April 1886. The Pryors were settled at *The Cottage*.

Temple Dinsley was then let to Mr and Mrs Frederick Macmillan - a name famous in the publishing world. Frederick was an uncle of the future Prime Minister, Harold Macmillan. The couple were settled there by October 1891 as Mrs Macmillan visited Preston School then. The couple took an interest in Preston's activities.

(Above, Temple Dinsley c.1880 - note the clock on the right)

Mr Macmillan *(left)* was Chairman of Preston Parish Council from 1894 until 1900. The couple were also involved in the building of St Martin's Church at Preston. The Macmillans left Preston in around 1900. It was noted in the school logbook that Mr Macmillan visited the school on 14 December 1899 to tell the pupils that they would have the Christmas Tree after the holidays, *'owing to his wife's illness'*. In 1901, Temple Dinsley was again vacant.

St Martin's Church, Church Lane - built (1899)

In 1849, the Dartons financed the construction of Preston Charity School at School Lane *(see page 36)*. From 1850, this new edifice for education doubled as a school on weekdays and a makeshift church on Sundays. This was no doubt seen as a means of keeping contact with the mother-church, St Mary of Hitchin. It required a special licence to perform a divine service in the school room which was granted by George, Lord Bishop of Rochester on 27 June 1850.

After the non-conformist *Bunyan's Chapel* was opened in 1877 - a building specifically dedicated to worship - there was a reaction from the Anglican community. In response to an approach by the vicar of St Mary, Ralston de Vins Pryor offered an acre of ground for the building of a new church and burial ground, provided enough funds could be raised to build it - though the need for a burial ground was debated. A subscription fund was set up and a folded contributions card was produced in August 1898 to record gifts. On its front page were listed the fund's committee: Rev. Canon Hensley, Rev. BN Switzer, FO MacMillan, Mrs MacMillan, Mrs Darton, English Harrison, RDV Pryor, and WO Times. There were fund raising activities like the concert organised by Frederick Armstrong of *Preston Hill Farm* which raised £11. The parish magazine noted: it is 'a matter for much congratulation that the inhabitants of Preston and their immediate friends have been instrumental in raising £500'. By January 1899 the church fund had reached almost £800. A design for the church (costed at £1,200) was submitted by TB Carter of 5 Staple Inn, London. The church was to seat 162 persons and it was finally agreed that 'the graveyard surrounding the church will be a great boon to Preston which till now has used Hitchin Cemetery for burials'.

The shortfall was quickly made up and on St Martin's Day, 11 November 1899, Mrs MacMillan laid the foundation stone. A procession consisting of the choirs of St Mary and St Martin, six clergy and about 250 people started from Preston School towards the site of the new church at noon. During the march, *The Church's One Foundation* was sung. On the conclusion of the ceremony, the procession returned to the school singing *All People that on Earth Do Dwell*.

The collections amounted to £11 2s 0d leaving £10 for the Building Fund after deduction for expenses. The weather was fine and pleasant, although somewhat windy.

St Martin was consecrated on 11 July 1900 at a ceremony attended by 600 worshippers, many of whom were gathered in what was designated to be the graveyard. *(Below are scenes from within the church, the lych-gate and the churchyard.)*

James Barrington-White at Temple Dinsley

James Barrington-White was Irish, having been born on 21 September 1856 at Orange Hill, Armagh, Northern Ireland. He held several prestigious posts in Armagh including being a member of the Committee of National Association of British and Irish Millers. In January 1898, James and Mary were living at Roxley Court, Willian, Herts. (a village near Hitchin). He then returned to Northern Ireland as he was appointed as the High Sheriff of Armagh. This meant that James was the English sovereign's *judicial* (as opposed to personal) representative, being responsible for law and order. By 1901, James was back in Hertfordshire for he bought the Temple Dinsley mansion, *The Cottage, Temple Farm* (with associated land) and two cottages at Preston Green. With this acquisition, he became Lord of the Manor of Temple Dinsley. He also purchased part of Wain Wood. Four years later, in 1905, he ordered the building of two semi-detached estate houses on the east side of Crunnells Green. These bore the inscription 'JBW 1905'. Perhaps reflecting his earlier judicial appointments, one of the houses (nearest Temple Dinsley) was for the village constable and had a lock-up in an attached outhouse. Later, the two cottages were joined and the resulting home is known today as *Crunnells Green Cottage (left)*.

In 1906, James had a mausoleum built at St Martin with a copper door and a Celtic cross – an echo of his Irish origins. His wife, Mary, was a Preston school manager. Mary died on 30 May 1914 at 15 Princesgate, London and was interred at St Martin on Tuesday, 2 June. James died twenty-one years later, aged seventy-nine, and was also interred behind the copper doors of the mausoleum on 21 February 1935. That he chose Preston to be his final resting ground is a measure of the regard that James had for the village. The couple lived in Preston for seven years.

The Seebohms at Poynders End

In 1903, the banker, Hugh Seebohm *(below)*, purchased the ninety-two-acre farm at Poynders End. Perhaps the 'very elevated position' of the farm which commanded 'views of several counties' made the property more appealing. He was the son of accredited economic historian Frederic Seebohm. Immediately, Hugh commissioned the architect, Geoffry Lucas of Hitchin, to design an 'Arts and Crafts' house to be built on his land *(below, bottom)*. This was completed in 1905. It is visible from the foot of Preston Hill.

Although Poynders End was considered to be a 'hobby farm', Hugh increased his holding by fifty acres as a result of two purchases in around 1911 and 1931. There is a pencilled note in the 1910 Inland Revenue Valuation Survey that he bought (3 and 4) Hitchwood Cottages. He then built 5 - 7 Hitchwood Cottages *(above)* in a style that complimented the design of Lutyen's cottages in the area.

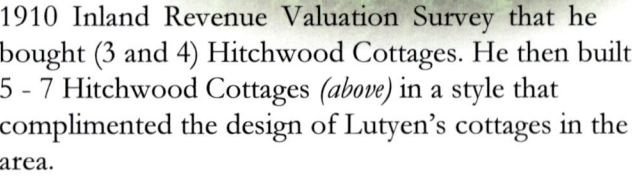

In his obituary, Seebohm was described as remaining 'to the end the traditional country banker. He was indeed essentially a countryman, finding his chief delight in himself and his farm and in this peaceful environment his love of trees and birds, of which his knowledge was profound'.

The Fenwicks buy Temple Dinsley

The Fenwicks were an established family of bankers in Northumberland during the nineteenth century. Herbert's grandfather, George, was a senior partner in Lambton's Bank and also had interests in hunting and was a director of the North Eastern railway. The Perkins family were associated with a major London Brewery and Charles Perkins (Violet's father) had interests in coal and iron, being a director of Consett Iron Company and owning coal mines in Northumberland.

Herbert George Fenwick was born at the Bristol Hotel, Edinburgh in 1870 and married Violet Edith Perkins on 14 August 1895 at Bolam Parish Church, Northumberland.

A few years later, in 1908, Herbert and Violet Fenwick bought Temple Dinsley. Almost immediately, Sir Edwin Lutyens was engaged to extend the mansion. As well as this construction programme, over the next five years or so the Fenwicks commissioned the building of several houses around Preston which were also designed by Lutyens.

This has produced a uniform feel to much of the architecture of the area. Thus, Preston's property stock was revitalised. The major source of the funding of these projects was provided by Violet Fenwick. It could therefore be argued that much of Preston's face owes it character to her.

It transpired that between 1908 and 1914, Herbert borrowed £26,300 to finance the 'Preston Project'. However, from around 1913, the relationship between Herbert and Violet became strained (which may be the reason that Violet ordered the building of *Hill End*). This culminated in their divorce in October 1917. During this time, Violet continued to live at Temple Dinsley.

It could be argued that much of Preston's face owes its character to Violet Fenwick.

On 30 June 1916, the full debt was transferred from Herbert to Violet. That same day, all of Herbert's holdings at Preston were also conveyed from Herbert to Violet. The deed notes, '...the hereditaments were purchased by the husband *at the request of the wife*' out of monies standing in their joint bank account and HGF's account...the greater part of which monies arose from the separate income of the wife' and 'the husband admits that the purchase monies...were satisfied wholly out of monies belonging to the wife'. As a result, Violet was the sole owner of the Temple Dinsley Estate. She sold the estate to Douglas Vickers on 24 May 1918.

Sir Edwin Lutyens at Preston

'The greatest *artist* in building whom Britain has produced' – thus, Sir Edwin Lutyens has been lauded. Edwin Landseer Lutyens was born on 29 March 1869 at Onslow Square, London. In 1885, he was sent to South Kensington School for Art. Four years later he was introduced to Gertrude Jekyll, doyen of English garden designers, a meeting which was to result in several architectural commissions.

Jekyll introduced Lutyens to those for whom she designed gardens and he planned architectural features for homes and gardens. The ultimate kudos for many wealthy families was a 'Lutyens house with a 'Jekyll garden' - 'Edwardian catch-words denoting excellence, something fabulous in both scale and detail'.

When studying for a gardening qualification, I was astonished to read of a Lutyens/Jekyll project at Preston. Jane Brown in *Gardens of a Golden Afternoon* mentions 'another good brick garden with elaborate terraces' at Temple Dinsley. She lists 'the rose garden with its elegant brickwork' as one of only twenty-four 'saveable' and 'hallowed' examples of the duo's work *(see page 33)*.

(*Above*) Temple Dinsley before the Lutyens' alterations; and after *(below)*

The rose garden at Temple Dinsley

c. 1911

c. 1911

c. 1911

Seen here are views of the rose garden planted by R Harkness beside the west wing of Temple Dinsley after it had been set out by Gertrude Jekyll 'one of the finest collaborations between Lutyens and Jekyll'. Below are two views from 2010. In the midst of the paved garden was Father Time, an old leaden figure, silvery-white and armed with a scythe and hour glass.

Today, Father Time has been replaced by a sun dial. The rose garden is acclaimed for its elegant brickwork. In 1981, a pupil who attended the Princess Helena College (PHC) described how the garden could still 'provide peace and seclusion' amidst the school girls. PHC today describes it as 'a stunning location for girls and staff to relax and for parents to enjoy at key school events'.

Above, are David *(left)* and Jonathan Fenwick painted in the rose garden by Annie Swynnerton in 1914. Right, are their nephew, Benedict Fenwick, and PHC Headmistress, Jo-Anne Duncan, in the rose garden a century later.

2010

2010

Buildings around Preston that were designed by Sir Edwin Lutyens

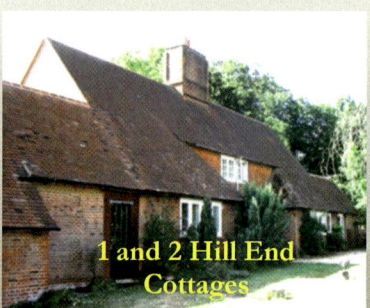

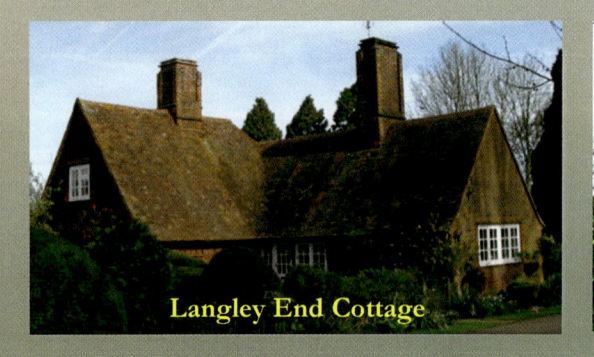

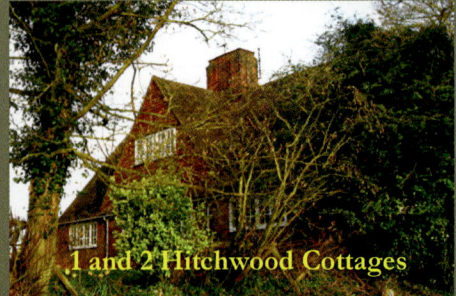

Ladygrove Farm

Crunnells Green House

Crunnells Green

Hill End

1 and 2 Hill End Cottages

Langley End Cottage

Ladygrove

Kiln Wood Cottage

1 and 2 Hitchwood Cottages

1 - 6 Chequers Cottages

Douglas Vickers at Temple Dinsley

Douglas Vickers *(left,)* (1861 – 1937) was an English industrialist and politician. He became a director of the family business in 1897 and was MP for Sheffield Hallam from 1918 until 1922. Vickers bought Temple Dinsley on 24 May 1918. He then supervised the building of *Crunnell's Green House* (pictured on the previous page) for the Estate Manager, Reginald Dawson (above, right), and the bungalows at School Lane *(below)*

The nearest bungalow was christened *The Institute Room*. It was presented to Mrs Vickers on her fiftieth birthday. She was President of the Women's Institute at the time.

Vickers created a herd of *Wessex Saddleback* pigs at *Castle Farm* and Reginald Dawson was the herdsman. In 1933, Pig Breeders' Annual stated that the herd was 'established in 1921 and that since then, upwards of 1,000 pigs had been reared each year'. From 1925, the herd received 500 awards at leading shows. The British Saddleback Breeders Club acknowledged that Reginald 'not only made Hertfordshire a strong centre (of *Saddlebacks*) but had done as much as any man for the breed'.
The Dawson's were considerably involved with the running of the village. Reginald was elected as Correspondent for Preston School on 19 May 1911 and was also a School Manager. In addition, he served as Chairman of Preston Parish Council from 1915 until 1937 and was a Herts. County Councillor. Reginald was also a keen cricketer. He was included in the 'Best-Ever Preston' team and was described as 'a driving force', a right-handed batsman and captain of Preston Cricket Club in the mid-1920's.

Almina, Countess of Carnarvon

Vickers put Temple Dinsley on the market in 1927 and it was purchased by Almina, Countess of Carnarvon. She was born on 14 April 1876 at Bayswater, London. Her mother was Marie Boyer, the daughter of a French financier from an old aristocratic family. Almina was a socialite who married the profligate fifth Earl of Carnarvon at Westminster in 1895.

The Earl had an interest in Egyptology. A combination of Carnarvon's optimism, Howard Carter's instincts and Alfred Rothchild's money helped them hit the jackpot: they found the tomb of Tutankhamun - 'golden beds and couches of state, golden caskets, chariots, candlesticks, furniture, statues, clothes, weapons and a magnificent throne, encrusted with gold, silver and jewels'. Carnarvon died and on 9 December 1923, Almina married Lieutenant Colonel Ian Dennistoun at a Registry Office at Princes Row. On 12 December 1929, *The Times* announced that the couple had 'arrived at Temple Dinsley, Hitchin, which is now their permanent address'. But they were often away from Preston.

However, transitory their life at Temple Dinsley, the couple became unhappy at the mansion. Perhaps they were not popular in the village – although an employee once described her as a 'kind employer'. She was noted as a 'somewhat eccentric lady who frightened the villagers by asking them to mount Tutankhamun relics on black velvet which naturally they refused to do.' Almina's interests lay 'chiefly elsewhere but her husband (who was not in the best of health) did much for Preston' and was a school manager.

In 1934, Almina and Ian moved to a new property on the Isle of Wight, however they retained some memories of Temple Dinsley as two of its fireplaces were dismantled and installed in their new home.
In April 1969, Almina, now aged 93, died in poverty. She (who dreaded swallowing fish and chicken bones) choked on a piece of gristle in a home-made chicken stew. It couldn't be dislodged so her lower esophagus was removed. Almina lingered for three weeks until her death.

Princess Helena College

Princess Helena College (PHC) was founded in 1820 and was later established at 32-33 Mornington Crescent, Hampstead. While having a wide syllabus, it had a narrow uptake of daughters of 'deceased Anglican Clergy and of Naval and Military Officers who had perished in the Napoleonic Wars'.

It was in 1875 that Queen Victoria's third daughter, Princess Helena, gave the school its title and PHC became a Public School. As a result, numbers gratifyingly swelled and a new, west London home was found for the college at Eaton Rise, Ealing. However, privacy became an increasing issue as London sprawled and the relative remoteness of Temple Dinsley at Preston was alluringly attractive.....

The move was made in 1935 after some alterations to the mansion. The 'upstairs' was converted into dormitories. Kitchen and dining rooms were installed and later the west wing roof was cranked up to provide still more accommodation. An art studio and music wing followed – the total cost of purchase and renovation being £48,712. After extensive renovation and the building of a new wing, in January 1992, the *Dower House* was opened as a new Sixth Form House.

For decades the College has deliberately integrated with the village, has provided considerable local employment (occasionally advertising positions in Preston's Parish Newsletter) and has allowed Preston folk to enjoy some of its facilities.

In recent years, PHC has opened its doors for several village functions such as the annual Preston Trust Supper; Friends of St Martin's events such as Barn Dances and Suppers; an annual Summer Ball; Family Fun Days; Christmas Fayres and Markets; Ladies Self-Defence Evenings; BBQs and hog Roasts; Jazz Lunches and Guy Fawkes Bonfires.

Education at Preston

The first Preston School is mentioned in the book, *Bringing Literacy to Rural England - The Hertfordshire Example* by J S Hurt. These are the facts about Preston's first school: it was united with the National Society on 14 January 1818. No grant from the National Society was recorded. It then withdrew from union with the National Society sometime between 1828 and 1832. It is probable that Elizabeth Darton was the guiding hand behind the forming of this school for the children of the village.

These dates are not necessarily when the school was built or demolished and the school was under the umbrella of the Anglican Church of St Mary, Hitchin. As it was administered by the National Society, Preston's School was neither a straw plaiting school nor a 'Dame' school. The Preston census of 1821 records Simon Stevens as a 'schoolteacher' - a position confirmed when some of his children were baptised. Perhaps, the quality of his instruction may be doubted - in the 1841 census he was noted as a farm worker and in 1851 he was living at Cocks Green, Kings Walden with his *labouring* son, Charles.

A new school built in 1849

In 1849, the incumbent Lord of the Manor, Thomas Darton, also showed a sense of guardianship and responsibility for the villagers. While his own children enjoyed the services of a personal governess (Eliza Forrester in 1851), apart from the plaiting schools, the local children of labourers had no provision for education. Mr Darton financed the construction of a rather austere and plain school building at what is today known as School Lane. The new school doubled as a church on Sundays from 1850.

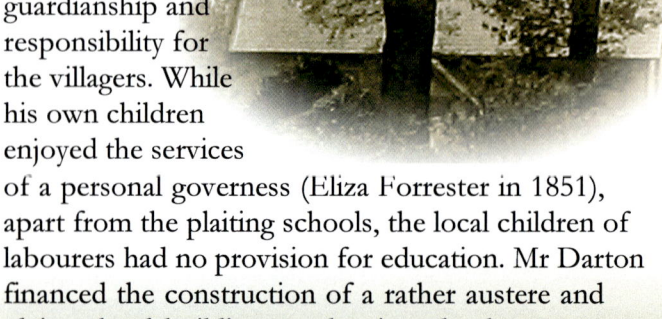

The School had two rooms. The main room was 40 feet long, 20 feet wide with a height of almost 15 feet to the plate. It had no ceiling and measured 24 feet 6 inches from the floor to the ridge of the roof. It was difficult to heat in winter, but a stove was provided, for which firewood was fetched and chopped. The windows in the schoolroom were deliberately sited so that the seated pupils were not distracted by glimpses of the outside world.

Preston's plaiting schools

As well as the Charity School, Preston had plaiting schools. In 1861, a plait school was recorded to the east of the village. A sketch map of Preston, dated 1884, shows two such schools: Mrs Peters' school at Preston Green and Mrs Stratton's school at Church Lane near *Bunyan's Chapel*.

The *Hertfordshire Mercury* included a note about these schools: 'Throughout Herts...plaiting schools are numerous and it is here that children are taught the art and (ostensibly) the three R's. The children remain at school at the usual school hours. Afterwards, during the time when they do not play, they plait a little till sent to rest. When they are about eight or nine years of age, they earn 2s - 3s a week.' In her book, *Labouring Life in the Victorian Countryside*, Pamela Horn wrote: 'The child, usually four years old was sent to a plait school. This was often little more than a child minding business held in a local cottage...their sole function was to keep the children working as hard as possible.'

Preston School Board, 1873

c. 1920

In 1873, Preston school had a new beginning. Following the Education Act of 1870, instead of being a Charity school, it was regulated by the state and subject to inspections to ensure standards were being maintained. With a flourish, the secretary (and school manager), Rev. Lewis Hensley, wrote in the opening page of the school log book, 'Mar 31 1873, Preston Church of England School opened under the charge of Miss Mary Jane Hyder - Certified Teacher'. Forty-six children were admitted. As more pupils attended the school, the main school room became inadequate. From 1880 the register recorded between seventy and ninety pupils. The report in 1884 referred to the 'cramped space' and in 1890 the 'very limited space' was noted.

Later the infants were taught in their own room. In 1881 there was a classroom measuring 10' 4" by 6' 4½". This was referred to as a 'small space' in 1892 and work began to enlarge the classroom in the following year. In 1897 it measured 18 feet (5.5m) by 16 feet (4.9m).

A Preston school classroom c. 1932

c. 1953

In 1953, Mrs Maybrick wrote, 'In 1947 it was found that there was not enough money to keep the school up to the standard required by the County Council, so the managers were faced with the alternative of closing down or taking a grant from the Council and becoming a 'Controlled' school. They decided that the children should be kept in the village up to the age of eleven so they signed an Instrument of Effect and the school became a Voluntary Primary (Controlled) School.'

A new Preston School in 1966

2010

The Headmaster's Report on Friday, 28 October 1966 began, 'The most important item being that they were at last in the new building (at Back Lane) and were delighted with it, staff, students and canteen staff alike'. The move took place in one day – the school moved after prayers in the old one on 12 October. There were fifty-one pupils.

The *Red Lion* at Preston Green

As can be clearly seen from its roof line, the *Red Lion* was originally two cottages. A study of the manorial records reveals that the cottages were built before 1664. As early as 1847, it was described as, 'An old established public house'.

With regard to the two cottages, that to the north was a small, 'one-up and one-down' type and its first floor room has a higher ceiling compared with the rooms of the larger house adjoining. From evidence discovered in the attics, the roof line of the smaller cottage was once lower and at some point the two houses were roofed to the same height.

Both cottages have been altered considerably over the years. However, the larger one still retains its typical nineteenth-century frontage with a modillioned eaves cornice and a range of three windows on the second floor, which have double hung sashes and glazing bars. In the attics, traces of the original wide floor boards can be seen in one bedroom and on the landing, while the other room on this level contains all of its eighteenth-century flooring.

An inglenook fireplace was discovered during recent alterations but all the fireplaces in both cottages have been considerably changed over the centuries. Two original windows on the first floor were found at the rear of the house. These had been hidden for many years after an extension was added in the nineteenth century.

A sizeable amount of land was attached to both cottages - three acres of pasture which lay behind the house and stretched into Back Lane. This land still belonged to the *Red Lion* until *Pryor House* was built and the new school was erected in Back Lane more recently. The field which lay by the side of the present footpath had been pasture for centuries, and consequently was the home of many rare wild flowers.

For more than a century, the Swain family owned the *Red Lion*. Then, Stephen Swain sold the inn to Joseph Saunderson in 1811. He farmed in a modest way and when he died in 1829, his wife, Harriet, took over the house and the land. This was on the understanding that the building and its contents would be auctioned on her death and the proceeds divided between their five children - Joseph, Sophia, Charles, Stephen and Alfred.

Harriet Saunderson supported herself and her family by farming and selling beer, for in 1832 she was listed in Piggott's Directory as a beer retailer. The premises was known as the *Lion* in 1844, and eventually as the *Red Lion*.

About 1844 Samuel Lucas, the brewers of Hitchin, came to an arrangement with her to supply beer. Mrs Saunderson died in 1847 and the property was put up for auction on July 24 of that year. It was described as having 'two sitting rooms, shop, tap room, kitchen, cellarage, five bedrooms, stabling, large garden, fruit trees and the common rights attached to it'.

The new owner was William Brown, a farmer from Bendish. The Brown family owned the *Red Lion* for 50 years and at first William and his wife Emma lived there with their four youngest children. Emma was a Preston girl and her husband was both publican and cattle dealer. (Their son, Frank is featured on page 105.) After about ten years they moved away and installed managers, for in 1846 Samuel and Ebenezer Foster were there. William Brown died in 1871 and his wife Emma and her son Alfred leased the public house to Messrs. Pryor Reid and Co of Hatfield in 1893. The tenants rented the property for £65 pa and the building was to be put in good order. This arrangement lasted for three years, for when his mother died at the age of over ninety, Alfred Brown sold the *Red Lion* to John Green, brewer of Luton, in 1897. The inn was acquired by Whitbreads in 1962.

Preston villagers buy the *Red Lion*

In the summer of 1980, Martin King, landlord of the *Red Lion*, died. His death was the catalyst for a turbulent period in the history of the Georgian pub.

Its owners, Whitbreads, decided that it should be sold. Ray Scarbrow, who managed the Luton pub, *The Somerset Tavern*, and *The Bull* at Gosmore, decided he could turn the *Red Lion* into a large steakhouse-style restaurant. He therefore applied for planning permission for building extensions to the pub, a fifty-vehicle car park and a forty-one-seater restaurant. These plans met with intransigent resistance from locals. A protest meeting that lasted two and a half hours was held at the village hall in August 1981. It was attended by most of the residents and chaired by Jack Raffell, the chairman of the parish council. Mr Raffell said, 'It's every village in North Herts. with a nice village green and a pretty area that is in danger. They are all under the same attack as we are now....If he (Mr Scarbrow) wants to keep on, we shall keep on and wear him down'.

The consensus was that Preston was a working village and needed a working village pub - not a roadhouse. Residents wanted a place where the cricket team, the darts team, the Hunt and the Morris dancers could meet and make merry. It was thought that the influx of outsiders to the restaurant would destroy the peace and charm of the village, cause noise late into the night and make the narrow lanes of the village a danger to children. New street lighting and pavements would spoil the character of The Green. Mr Scarbrow said, 'It is an eyesore as it is. It is a pub that has been let go and is in desperate need of having money spent on it. The villagers will say they are all using it, but they are not. The trading figures show they are not'. The area planning committee met in the Council Offices, Grammar School Walk, Hitchin, where one hundred people crowded into a small committee room.

It emerged that the planners had been informed that the Secretary of State for the Environment had decided to make the *Red Lion* a statutory listed building. This meant that as well as obtaining planning permission for the alterations, an application for listed building consent would also have to be heard. However, the listing of the pub was to have implications later. The committee unanimously refused the application.

Having secured their victory, would villagers who were prepared to put protesting pens to paper now be prepared to put their hands in their pockets? The *Red Lion* was priced at £125,000. A further £10K was needed for initial operating expenses. £95K was raised in Preston and a bank loan of £40K covered the shortfall. The response of locals laid to rest any doubts about what Preston thought of their pub.

Renovations under way

All villagers living within three miles of the *Red Lion* had the right to own shares if it was their wish. All but a handful of the 130 Preston households took up their right, contributing between £1 and several thousands of pounds. This was important as Whitbread's had sought a reassurance that at least 80% of the householders would be involved including voting rights.

With jubilant celebrations, the *Red Lion* re-opened on 19 March 1983 - the final touches having been completed at around 05.00. Preston now possessed its own working pub. It was the first community-owned pub in Great Britain.

The Chequers inn

Today, *The Chequers* is a private house, but for centuries it was an inn. It was built in the seventeenth century or even earlier. In 1788, it was referred to as *Cheker*s. Traditionally the inhabitants of Chequers Lane frequented their nearest public house. For many years, *The Chequers* was part of the Temple Dinsley estate and its occupants were tenants of the manor. Until 1926, Temple Dinsley manorial courts were held there.

John Young, the victualler there in 1784, was succeeded by his son who also worked as a gamekeeper on the estate. The Young family lived at *The Chequers* for over sixty years and in 1841 John and Ann Young were there with their five sons, the eldest working as a wheelwright. At some time during the next ten years they moved away and by 1851 Henry Bradden and his wife Rebecca ran the public house.

During this period, the Dartons of Temple Dinsley leased *The Chequers* to W & S Lucas, a brewing family of Hitchin. When Henry McLean Pryor purchased Temple Dinsley in 1873, the public house, stable and barn was rented by Lucas for £30 pa. In May the following year the licence was transferred to William Jeeves, who became the new manager of *The Chequers*. Some years later his wife Mary died, leaving him to care for their five children. He continued to run the public house until December 1891, having been there for over 17 years.

W & S Lucas, had continued to renew their tenancy and in 1900 Henry Pryor gave them a twenty-one-year lease at £55 pa. By the time this had expired there was a new owner at Temple Dinsley, Douglas Vickers, and the Hitchin brewers obtained a further lease of ten years for £40 pa.

After World War One, the Lucas family sold their business to J. W. Green of Luton.

Although it was agreed that the Lucas' inns would continue to run separately, by 1923 the Hitchin Brewery was closed down and its licensed houses were merged with those of Greens. That same year when the lease was terminated Douglas Vickers sold *The Chequers* to J. W. Green who had in turn amalgamated with Flowers of Stratford-on-Avon. By 1959, Flowers disposed of the orchard attached to *The Chequers* and closed down the public house. Sadly, the empty building was vandalized and set on fire. Fortunately it was not damaged beyond repair as it is one of the oldest and most attractive hoses in the village. In 1960, *The Chequers* was purchased by Thomas Bertram Daltry, a solicitor by profession. He made a covenant with the brewers not to carry on any licensed trade at the premises as Flowers still controlled the *Red Lion* on the Green. Since that time, *The Chequers* has been carefully restored to reveal its ancient timbers and inglenook fireplaces. There are two cellars, one with an unusual barrel roof. Old photographs indicate that it was, at one time, two cottages while building work in the 1970s uncovered that a third cottage once lay behind the house.

(Above) Maggie Whitby nee Wray at *The Chequers* c.1929

Preston once had a third public house - the *Horse and Groom*. Its owners, Marshall and Pierson, were brewers at Hitchin. It is first mentioned in the Hitchin Rate Book of 1838. When William Simpson auctioned the *Horse and Groom* it was described as having a tap room, parlour, bar, cellar and several bedrooms. There were also stables and outhouses, a yard and garden (when Henry Darton bought the beer shop for £400). The buildings stood on the corner of the Green *(shown below)*.

Strawplaiting

> According to the census of 1851, there were ninety-seven straw plaiters in Preston ranging from children aged three to the widow, Jane Fairey (73). Sixty years later, in 1911, there was not a single plaiter. What was straw plaiting? Why did it flourish at Preston and then decline?

The country craft of straw plaiting involves twisting together lengths of straw (as one would braid hair) to produce interwoven lengths in different and intricate patterns *(some are shown below)*. Young and old, women and men, were straw plaiters. Children were taught how to plait at plaiting schools. Finished work was sold at a plait market or to a plait dealer who then supplied manufacturers of products such as straw hats and bonnets. The craft was practised mainly in the counties of Hertfordshire, Bedfordshire, Buckinghamshire and Essex.

The voracious demand for straw plait was fuelled by a fashion change from the cotton mob hats of the eighteenth century to the straw bonnets of the 1800s. Even when the English plaiting industry had been undercut by cheap imports at the end of the nineteenth century, the straw boater was still essential summer wear.

Watch grainy film of the announcement of the Armistice in 1919 and wonder at the number of straw hats being launched into the air like so many frisbies.

Why did Hertfordshire become a centre of straw plaiting? The county produced excellent quality straw and from the mid-1850s, superior varieties of wheat such as *Red Lammas*, *Rivet* and *Golden Drop* were introduced. These strains thrived on the Chiltern fields of chalk such as those around Preston. Their straw was curiously 'valued in the inverse ratio of the vigour of the plant' – the best straw came from the poorest areas - and contained enough silico to be strong, but not brittle.

Another factor was the availability of manure. It was accepted good husbandry to plough straw into the fields to maintain their fertility. This was considered to be so important that landowners stipulated that their tenant farmers could not sell off their straw. However, manure was an alternative fertiliser and there was a constant supply of this from thousands of stables in London (which was less than forty miles away) to Hertfordshire. It was laid down that a ton of straw could be sold to the plaiters for every two cart loads of muck brought in by farmers.

When the average Hertfordshire agricultural wage was between 10s and 12s a week, straw plaiting wives could earn more than their husbands - and even the contributions of children to the family income-pot were considerable. However, there were social repercussions as a result of this extra source of income. Arthur Young wrote, 'The farmers complain of it as doing mischief for it makes the poor saucy and no servants can be procured or any field work done where this manufacture establishes itself'.

How straw was plaited

Wheat for straw plaiting was carefully reaped – and a little earlier than the rest of the harvest. After the cut, suitable straws for plaiting were selected by a drawer. Only perfect samples that were not diseased or rain-spattered were chosen.

After the ears were lopped off, the resulting 56lb bundles were sold to plait dealers who cut the straw into usable lengths and then sorted it into different thicknesses using a wooden trough with metal circles *(shown right)*.

41

The graded straw was tied into small sheaves, perhaps bleached and dyed and sold to dealers or directly to plaiters for 4d, 6d, 8d or 10d according to the quality of the straw and state of the market. A further reason that English straw became usable rather than Tuscany imports was that at the turn of the seventeenth century an efficient method of splitting the straw into narrow splints was found, using a 'splitter' which cost only one or two pennies *(see below)*. A cone funneling into a set of cutters was pushed into the end of a straw. This split the straw into a number of roughly equal pieces.

The plaiter worked by interweaving three straws in front of her hands and allowing the finished braid to drop towards the body. A bundle of moistened straws was pinned under her left arm pit. As she worked, she would bend her head and pull out one or two new straws, moistening them with saliva and then storing them on the sides of her mouth ready to be plaited. The corner of her lips might be scarred or coloured as a result. Teeth might rot. It was said, 'Never kiss a plaiter!'.

Like casting-on knitting, starting the plait was demanding, as was adding new splits – if a plait was wide, replacing straws was almost continuous. Plaiters were taught to use their thumb and second finger, using their forefinger to turn the splint:

'Under one; and over two.
Pull it tight; and that will do'.

When the plait was completed, the ends and beginnings of the straw protruded until they were clipped off. It was essential to keep the ends of the plait damp, so in wintertime women sat away from the fire and kept warm by filling an earthenware pot with embers or coals and placing the pot under their skirt.

An accurate guide of the length of a plait were notches cut in mantelpieces at increments of nine, eighteen inches and a yard. Work was sold in multiples or fractions of a 'score' (i.e. twenty yards).

The plait was now ready for the 'brimstone boxes'. These were large, but light – an old fashioned clothes box was ideal. The plait was placed in the middle of the box leaving a clear space in the middle. Then, a saucer or tin lid with a small live coal was placed in the space and a piece of brimstone was balanced on the coal for fumigating or 'steaming'. Thus, the plait was bleached, giving it a brighter appearance.

The routine of a plaiter

An insight into plaiting at Preston in around 1870 is given by Edwin Grey of Harpenden, Herts. (which is ten miles from Preston). He wrote, 'Very many of the women and girls were engaged in it (straw plaiting): some of the men and lads were also good at the work, doing it at odd times, or in the evening after farm work, but this home industry was always looked upon as women's work...and (male) plait hardly ever came up to the standard of that made by women....some men and lads who although not good at making any of the finer sorts, would make the rough and coarser plait called 'whole straw'. This as the name implies is made from whole unsplit straw. I've known men and boys when home from the farm early in winter, or on wet days, sit and make many yards of this coarser material, but this variety when all finished off and ready for sale, realised but a few pence per score yards...very little of the plait made by men or children was taken to the open market. That which was of use being bought up by plait buyers who came round weekly'.

The industry was most suitable for cottagers. It was clean and the housewife could, when wanting to go on with other house-work, put aside her plaiting, resuming it again at any time. She could also do the work sitting in the garden or whilst standing by the cottage door enjoying a chat or gossip with her neighbours. A mother could rock the cradle with her foot whilst using both hands at the plaiting. In summer-time when strolling in the lanes or fields they would often be plaiting. Most of the plaiters became so clever that they could do the work quickly, setting in their straws or splints and then finishing off the same with hardly a glance at it, for they could tell by the feel of the fingers when a new splint was required for insertion. Some workers' fingers become quite sore and bleeding because of working so hard to get the required yards of plait finished.

Plaiting at Preston

The first historical references to 'The Plait' at Preston are in the Hitchin Parish Registers of 1816/17 when Edward Willmott of Sootfield Green was described as a 'plait dealer'.

In the census of 1841, John Day was also noted as a 'plait dealer'. According to the census, there were ninety-seven plaiters at Preston in 1851. The seventeen males at the craft in the village were all aged under twelve.

In its heyday of 1861, there were one hundred plaiters recorded at the village – out of a population of 424. They included Ann Walker (76) and William Fairey (5). Ten years later, Preston had sixty-five plaiters including Mary Scott (65) and Lizzie Fairey aged four.

Although a second school for 'proper' education had been established at Preston in 1849, as noted earlier the 1861 census notes a plaiting school between Poynders End and Kiln Wood House. Also, a sketch map of Preston dated 1884 (fourteen years after compulsory education had been introduced - so children probably attended plait school after official school hours) shows two centrally-located plaiting schools run by Mrs Elizabeth Stratton (who was running a plait school in 1871) and Mrs Sarah Peters. It is worth noting that when both ladies married they marked the marriage certificate rather than signing and so were probably illiterate.

In fair weather, mothers would take their older children with them for the three-mile trek to sell their work at the Hitchin plait market *(shown below)*. It was a long tramp but the tedium was relieved as old friends were met on the road. The journey back home was harder than the outward trip - usually the goods carried back home were heavier than the plait and the women were tired after their exertions. If the weather was bad, Grey said he had seen 'women return in a very pitiable plight'.

Why 'The Plait' died out

The number engaged in the craft at Preston had dropped by 1881 to thirty-four plaiters. The only child aged fourteen or under who was plaiting was Arthur Palmer (12) – the rest were at school. There were just twelve plaiters in 1891; thirteen in 1901 and none in 1911.

Many parents wanted their children to plait because they contributed to the family's income. They could earn up to 6d a day when the father was earning about 10 shillings a week. To offset the accusation of the exploitation of child labour, it has to be said that 'the Plait' meant that widows and physically incapacitated people could support themselves through plaiting rather than throwing themselves upon parish relief. At Preston the censuses of 1851 and 1861 record only two people as receiving relief. But the main benefit was that family could enjoy a higher standard of living than in other rural parts because of women and children's earnings as plaiters.

When areas of England were embroiled in uprisings due to discontent at low rural wages (such as the Swing Riots of the 1830s), Hertfordshire was relatively peaceful - only one serious case was dealt with arising from the Farm Labourers' Revolt. The lid was kept on the bubbling pot of rebellion in the county - thanks in part to 'the Plait'. There were other social spin-offs. The independence of women had become an issue and even attitudes towards illegitimacy were affected as women were able to support themselves. Why depend on an unloved man earning a relatively low income? The situation of my great grandmother, Mary Currell, may illustrate this: although undeniably poor, in 1881 she headed a household of seven which was supported by three female straw plaiters.

The straw that broke the camel's back was the Education Act of 1870 which ordered the compulsory school attendance of children. For many years 'the Plait' was probably the difference between poverty and a tolerable standard of living for many Preston households.

Crime at Preston

Preston, like most villages, was peaceful in the nineteenth century. As a small community, everyone was aware of the 'goings-on' and effectively policed their neighbours - so there were few opportunities for serious crime. Cases of poaching, drunkenness, petty theft, arson and assault in the village occasionally troubled the magistrates at Hitchin. But unlike other areas, the villagers did not rise up in protest at low wages during the Swing Riots of the 1830s - possibly due to the assuaging effect of their plaiting income, as already noted.

The sentences meted out for petty crime took into account the good behaviour or otherwise of the defendants. A typical fine for poaching was 10s including costs - about a week's wages. But, in December 1860, a 17-year-old and a 20-year-old man from Back Lane were charged with setting snares. As they had been committed only a fortnight earlier for a similar offence, they were sent to a House of Correction for one month each. Offenders were usually fined with costs or imprisoned by default. Many either preferred a short spell in gaol or could not afford to pay the fine.

The most notorious local crime was the 'Preston Hill Case' of January 1864 *(see page 83)*.

The fight against lawlessness was stepped up in 1856 when Parliament passed the County and Borough Police Act. This made professional rural constabularies compulsory. The constables, knowing the lie of the land and the lawbreakers in their community, were far more likely to 'collar the criminals'. In 1871 and 1881, Preston had its own constables living in the village, Daniel Farr and then Abel Day.

The constable would patrol the muddy or dusty lanes on the off-chance that he would come across an 'incident' which would enliven his day. It was tedious work - bringing boredom and blisters - but the sight of his top hat bobbing above hedges would alarm the guilty. Constables were paid between 16s and 21s a week (rather more than a labourers wage), and were provided with a free uniform. From 1873, they received a boot allowance which acknowledged their tiresome trudging. To illustrate their work, in December 1871, PC Farr was walking from Preston to Ley Green one Saturday afternoon when he saw two men whom he knew and suspecting they were 'up to no good', he watched them.

He saw them take up and set snares and found a ferret concealed in their clothes. On another occasion, in 1870, he found a local 21-year-old Preston man on the road with a gun and after a search, he found powder and shot in his possession.

Poaching

Poaching was widespread in Preston, even in the twentieth century. I have found forty-six reported examples of Preston men being accused of poaching between 1841 and 1888. These were the tip of the iceberg.

Because of low wages, the temptation to catch or shoot game which ran or flew tantalizingly nearby and add it to the cook-pot was alluring. One of my uncles, who occasionally fell upon hard times and received parish relief, expressed this attitude - 'I'm not going to starve when (the local gamekeeper) Harper's got all those'. This feeling was not frowned upon by sympathetic villagers. After drinking at his pub, my father often regaled us with stories of his poaching.

But there was also the mind-set that poaching was a exciting contest and a battle of wits between the poacher and the police and gamekeepers. One poacher said of his pastime, '...once begun, no goen back - it get hold of you'. He said that the excitement soothed his conscience (if it troubled him) and spoke of his satisfaction in having 'the Keepers and Police beat' - which went a long way towards recompensing for the danger and risk. Perhaps this was the reason that some believed that poaching led a man 'step by step to almost every other crime'.

The Game Laws were resented and created friction between landowners and labourers. According to the Game Act (1831), there were two categories of day-time poaching - killing game without a certificate (£5 fine) and trespass in search of game (max. £2 fine). Night-time poaching was a more serious offence. In 1862, the power of search was given to the police by the Poaching Prevention Act ('a black day for the labourer') which was still in force in the late twentieth century.

The Act allowed the search of anyone suspected of poaching or of having equipment (such as a net, snares or gun) which could be used to take game. This, like the 'Stop and Search' powers recently given to the police, caused great resentment. As a result of searches, other pilfered items such as wood and turnips might be discovered.

Petty theft

Other offences committed by villagers included petty larceny - for example, theft of a bundle of wood, turnips, a truss of straw and half a bushel of coleseed tops (or rape). In 1841, Mary Ward and Elizabeth Thredder, two girls, aged about twelve and sixteen, were charged with stealing turnips. The turnips were growing in a field occupied by Mr John Cook of Hill End.

In February 1843, George Fairey was indicted for stealing a rabbit pudding and a pudding cloth, the property of Henry Bradden of *The Chequers*. Rebecca Bradden, said that Fairey 'came into the taproom and had a pint of beer. I had a rabbit pudding cooking on the fire. I went out of the room and heard a rattling, but took no notice of it. After Fairey came out, I went back when I found the pudding gone out of the pot. A man, John Day, afterwards came in and I went after Fairey. I found him in the field, asleep, and by his side the pudding cloth and some bones.'

Drunkenness

Excessive drinking was common among working men, who were accustomed to being fuelled by 'small beer' as they worked, instead of drinking unhygienic water from ditches and ponds. Several cases involving Preston labourers came before Hitchin magistrates. For example, a Preston man was charged with being drunk and riotous at Gosmore by PC Day. He failed to appear at court and was later found drunk again at Hitchin market. He was fined 2/6d and 16/6d costs.

Assault

There were several cases of assault by Preston men. Many fights predictably took place at public houses and Preston Fair. Farmers also seemed keen to take the law into their own hands as they saw fit. In August 1873, farmer George Wright, was summonsed for having assaulted a young woman, Mary Slater. Mr Shepherd appearing for the accused said the defendant 'was exceedingly sorry.... but since the occurrence a satisfactory arrangement had been come to between himself and the complainant's father and the young woman did not now wish to press the charge.' Then, in December 1870, Wright was further charged with assaulting one of his labouring boys, Samuel Reeves (11, a plough boy), who appeared in court 'with his arm very much injured'. Fined £3.

Highway offences

Various offences under this heading were common: riding without reins; negligent driving; obstructing the highway; leaving a horse and cart unattended; driving unlighted vehicles; allowing cattle to stray onto the highway to feed them and neglecting to repair an assigned stretch of road.

Domestic strife

Preston families had their domestic differences such as the twenty-six-year-old man (not the Sharpest tool in the box) who stabbed his father at Preston Green. There was an altercation at Back Lane in September 1877 when a 20-year-old woman assaulted a fifteen-year-old boy. Another case involved a wife who separated from her husband. He later refused to maintain her. She and her parents returned to the cottage at Preston Hill and removed all of the furniture and other items. A list of items taken was read out in court to the amusement of all. In January 1842, Robert Thrussell was fined 5/- for a brutal assault upon his wife, Martha, who was in a very far advanced state of pregnancy. Being unable to pay the fine, he was committed to the gaol at Hertford for two months.

"I should say that the village and indeed the whole of the parish was...free from any serious crime"

Arson

Arson was a capital offence until 1837 and there were five cases reported at Preston. The attraction of fire-raising was not only the thrill of combustion and witnessing the resulting charge of the Hitchin horse-drawn fire engine but sometimes incendiarism was a way of settling old scores or even making a social protest. In April 1860, a forty-eight-year-old Preston labourer was accused of setting fire to a wheat stack at *Stagenhoe Bottom Farm* and a year later a Luton man was sentenced to seven years penal servitude for arson at *Castle Farm*.

Juvenile crime

There was some juvenile misbehaviour in Preston. The domestic stabbing mentioned earlier was the result of a boy 'hooting' at a slow-witted young man. There were two cases of ill-treatment to animals by juveniles: three young men threw stones at a pig, breaking a leg and two boys aged eleven and nine 'ill-treated a lamb by riding it and beating it with a stick whereupon it died'. One of the boys was whipped.

An impression from trawling the news reports in the nineteenth century, is that a number of different labourers from Preston were involved in petty crime. The village had its 'problem families' and there were some incorrigible 'repeat' offenders. However, a contemporary first-hand report about crime at Harpenden (which is twelve miles from Preston) probably describes Preston well: 'I should say that the village and indeed the whole of the parish was...free from any serious crime, for I can remember nothing more startling than an occasional poaching affray, or a fowl stealing case, a public house fight, a neighbour's squabble or maybe a few cases of petty theft.....Our police force at this time consisted of one man'. *(Edwin Grey)*

Morality and Preston villagers

Even today, this sensitive subject may be distressing and frowned upon by many, especially older ones. But one cannot change the bald facts of life which involve one's forefathers, however untenable. Many family histories have instances of pregnant brides and illegitimacy - indeed, were it not for the loose morals of several of my ancestors, I should never have been born. Who am I to be judgemental!

Two main topics have been researched: bridal pregnancy and illegitimacy (that is, children born out of wedlock). I have a non-salacious interest in this subject as, to put it bluntly, several of my family at Preston were fornicators and I wondered how they would have been regarded by their neighbours.

Pregnant brides at Preston

How many of Preston's brides were 'infanticipating' as they walked (or waddled) up the aisle of local churches? It is a simple exercise to check when a couple married against the baptismal date of the first child born to the newly-weds. These details can be found on the Preston History web site. During the century between 1800 and 1900, out of 117 brides who remained in Preston after their wedding, thirty-six were pregnant (31%). This is unremarkable. The ratio conforms to the national average - 'in the first half of the nineteenth century almost one-third of all brides were pregnant'.

The pulpits of Anglican and Baptist churches resounded with dire warnings and cautionary tales of the folly of fornication.

Despite these flashing red lights, there would appear to be a general acceptance among the labouring classes of Preston that courting couples could be intimate before their nuptials or that, if an unmarried girl became pregnant, her partner would 'do the right thing'. The local couple, who left their marriage to the latest of last minutes in the nineteenth century, were married at St Mary, Hitchin, on 9 December 1844 and quietly baptised their first child twenty-nine days later at Kings Walden on 7 January.

"There would appear to be a general acceptance among the labouring classes of Preston that courting couples could be intimate before their nuptials"

Illegitimacy

In the Church's eyes, those children born out of wedlock were frowned upon. Illegitimacy has been described as 'an offence of the poor and the obscure'. Such progeny were often stigmatised in the parish records - one author listed eighty-seven different words, horrible, staining words in English and Latin, that were used to identify the fruits of fornication.

Because it was likely that a financial burden might be placed on the parish following the birth of a child to a single woman, a Maintenance Order might be issued. The father was instructed to make a payment to the overseers of the poor to offset the costs of confinement and care of the infant, as happened to Charles Swain of Preston in 1808.

According to the baptismal records of Hitchin, Kings Walden and Ippollitts (which include Preston people), out of 859 baptisms, thirty-four were illegitimate (4%) – that is, no father is noted on the page. This is slightly lower than the national average which was about 6% in the middle of the 1800s. Only two of these children died in infancy. Although fewer children were baptised near the end of the nineteenth century, there was a slight trend towards greater illegitimacy in later decades.

Local case studies

An extraordinary example of immorality at Preston concerned my great grandmother, Mary Currell (nee Fairey). Her first child, my grandmother Emily, was born almost four years before Mary married her husband, Thomas Currell. When at last the couple tied the knot they had four more children. However, when the 1881 census was taken, Thomas was no longer living with the family. Then, in 1884, Mary, aged 42, had a son baptised whose father was not recorded in the baptismal register.

With this flagrant parental example set before them, it is hardly surprising that Mary's daughters (who were aged seven and ten in 1882 and so witnessed her behaviour with knowing eyes) should also have illegitimate children. One was born at Brighton, which may show a desire to conceal the birth from the prying eyes of villagers.

Earlier in the century, there was another similar example of a mother and her daughter having illegitimate children. The family were living firstly in one of *Preston Hill Farm's* cottages and then at Kiln Wood. Both mother and daughter had three illegitimate children. In the mother's household from 1841 to 1861 there is a male lodger of a similar age and one wonders whether they were in a common-law marriage.

Conclusion

Because of the prevalence of premarital sex, especially among the labouring class, it is hard to believe that pregnant brides would have been looked down upon by their peers - although in a small village they might have been the butt of gossip and speculation. Possibly, immorality was less socially acceptable as the rate was below the national average. It would have been difficult to hide an extra-marital affair in such a tightly-knit community.

Movement and mobility

When researching the mobility of Preston villagers, a distinction should be made between the 'locals' and newcomers. Included among the new arrivals were many farmers who had no roots in the area, their transient farm servants and tradesmen's apprentices. Several of these temporary residents suddenly appear at Preston in one census and vanish without trace ten years later. I have therefore concentrated on people who were renting cottages around Preston when looking at their movements.

The historian, David Hey, in his book, *Journeys in Family History* states, 'Although people were strongly attached to their own parish, they also felt that they belonged to a wider, more loosely-defined district which they thought of as their "country" - the neighbourhood that was bounded by the nearest market towns'.

He then reminds us that people had a sense of belonging to a neighbourhood in which they 'had friends and relations who spoke like they did and who earned their living in the same familiar ways'. He added that ordinary men and women married someone from their own 'country'.

Much of this was true of Preston villagers in the nineteenth century. As we will see, most were born either in Preston or within a five mile radius of the village and remained inside this area taking marriage partners from the vicinity. When researching marriages of Preston folk, the same familiar names of local families reoccur like old friends.

However, there was less of an attachment to their own *parish* here than is suggested, perhaps because of the way in which the parish boundaries dissected Preston. Villagers (apparently with little regard to parish loyalty) moved from and went to Kings Walden, Ippollitts, St Pauls Walden, Kimpton, Offley and other nearby parishes.

One of the obstacles to freedom of movement between parishes was the Poor Law arrangements whereby newcomers to an area were discouraged if they posed a potential drain on local resources because of illness, unemployment or poverty. The worst case scenario would be a single mother with children moving into a parish, with all the implications for their future care. Probably, she would be quickly dispatched or 'removed' to her settled parish by the overseers. Because of the straw plaiting activities of old and young women and children in Hertfordshire, perhaps there was less concern about the burden they might place on local finances. In Preston, from 1851 - 1901, only eleven people were described as 'pauper' or 'receiving parish relief' in the censuses.

As a result of this extra income, movement between parishes in Hertfordshire did not pose too many problems for the local parish overseers. Another factor which should be considered when researching the mobility of Preston villagers is how far the agricultural labourers were prepared to walk to the farms on which they worked. There are few indicators of where they worked, but newspaper reports indicate that labourers did not necessarily live near their work. For example, during a court case in 1882, Thomas Jeeves, who kept the *Bull Inn* at Gosmore, produced an alibi that he was working at Temple Dinsley, about a mile away. Also, in 1876, Charles Watson, a farm labourer who lived in Hitchin, was working for Mr Marriott at *Castle Farm*, Preston, which was almost three miles from his home.

> The chart shown right illustrates how the population of Preston decreased during the nineteenth century - from 458 in 1841 to 318 in 1901. There were also fewer homes *(red blocks, right)* - 82 in 1851; 64 in 1901. A significant drop in both figures occurred when the *Preston Hill Farm* cottages were demolished circa 1870.

- Still at Preston
- In Herts.
- Unknown
- Away from Herts.
- Within 5 miles of Preston

1841 - 1851   1871 - 1881   1891 - 1901

The arrival of the railway at Hitchin also pushed back barriers to travel and mobility. In 1864, when the robber of a dying man at the bottom of Preston Hill went on the run, he took the train from Hitchin to Hatfield which is fourteen miles away. In the 1890s, the children of Preston were able to enjoy two day trips to the seaside. One excursion was to Skegness which was eighty-seven miles away.

Using the 1841 census as a starting point, of the 392 local people living in Preston (excluding farmers and their servants), exactly 200 (51%) were born in the village. Furthermore, another 102 were born within five miles of the village, principally at Kings Walden - thus more than three-quarters of Preston's population then were born within a five-mile radius of the village.

Between 1841 and 1901, from figures extracted from the censuses, 983 (52%) local people moved out of Preston - but they didn't move far. Of these, 387 (39%) relocated within five miles of the village and a further 295 (30%) stayed within the county of Hertfordshire. One hundred and three relocated to the town of Hitchin and approximately fifty moved to London.

The young blood of the village was seeping away ... this 'English village began to rot from the centre'.

Snapshots taken between 1841 and 1901 reveals that the trend was for young couples and their children to move from Preston and this continued well into the twentieth century. The young blood of the village was seeping away - in common with many others, this 'English village began to rot from the centre'.

1841 1851 1861 1871 1881 1891 1901 1911

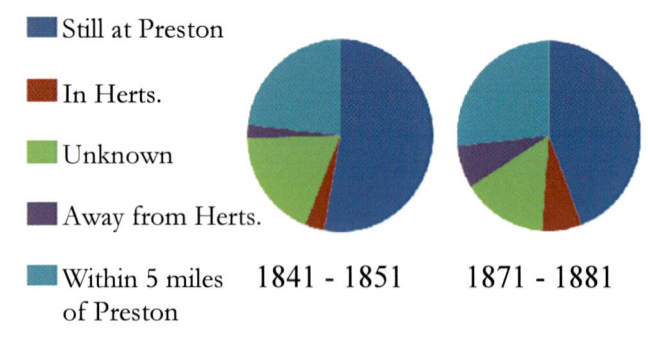

> The charts on the left show where people living at Preston one year, were living ten years later - and whence they moved. They indicate that there was a consistent exodus from the village of around half of the population over sixty years.

Why did people leave Preston? It has been suggested that there was an understandable desire to earn better wages than farm labourers could command - hence the shift to towns such as Hitchin, Luton and London. While this was undoubtedly the case for a few villagers, the majority moved to other parts of the countryside and continued as agricultural labourers.

Perhaps the two fundamental reasons for families leaving Preston were that, firstly, the farms could not provide the sheer volume of work for so many men and secondly (and even more basically), there were just not enough houses in the village in which young adults and children could live. The censuses indicate that the number of homes in Preston decreased by eighteen between 1851 and 1901. Faced with no work or homes, young couples packed their belongings, arranged for the services of a carter and left.

Lanes and highways

If the highways of the town of Hitchin were in a claggy state in the seventeenth century, the country lanes around Preston were mud-bound and impenetrable in wintertime. The problem was created by Preston topography – the chalky sub-soil prevented free drainage and the clay top-soil was easily churned into a quagmire.

It must have been high summer in 1890 that Griggs travelled along the lane from Charlton to Preston. He wrote, 'From there to Preston, uninterrupted and unchanged, the lovely grassy way stretched. No art could design anything so utterly charming. It was a place for loitering and meditation, or for enjoyment of the views it afforded whenever it rose from its hollow snugness into prominence on a hillside...From Gosmore on to Preston the scene, as I remember it, was one of *white road* (my italics) and green fields, hedges and trees, with hints of blue horizons. There was no house between them.'

In the early 1700s, villagers living at the end of impassable lanes complained that they were 'weary of this deep dertie country life' (sic). Although the lanes were called 'thoroughfares', few were able to 'fare' through as winter devoured 'whatsoever we were able to lay on in the summer'. A petition raised in 1726 read: 'so bad and ruinous are (the byways) and so narrow that the waggoners cannot in some parts go on the outside of the cart ruts and several dismal accidents have lately happened'. Mr Hale of Kings Walden faced with the obstacle course which was his run via Preston to Hitchin invented a one-wheel cart which slotted between the ruts. When Benedict Ithell of Temple Dinsley ordered a new carriage, its makers asked for the width of the ruts in his area so that his carriage's wheels could be set precisely that distance apart.

The surveyors of highways were constantly ordering repairs: 'pecking in the ruts' or filling holes with faggots or stones and then ploughing the road. Then, in 1767, Robert Hinde wrote to a surveyor:

The straightened road at Preston Hill c. 1920

'I must not only desire but insist that you will directly give orders that the roads leading to Hitchin may be made passable – which at present they are not. I was in the most imminent danger of being overturned the last time I went to Hitchin, which prevents my going ever to Church.' Another time he referred to the 'tortuous, pitch-dark and perilous tracks to Preston' which made it impossible to venture out after nightfall (unless one was a highwayman) and added, 'your ancestors contrived our narrow lanes in the days of wheelbarrows before those great engines, carts, were invented'. Largely as a response to Hinde's grumblings, a new highways officer was appointed and efforts were made to improve the infrastructure. The officials of Preston reported, 'We have made search (according) as our (office) requires and find all things well. As for the highways they are passable.'

Further work near Preston village was carried out in 1817: 'Ordered that the surveyors of Preston hamlet should repair the highway between Preston Green and Dead Woman's Lane by raising the same in the centre with stones and by making drains on each side to carry off the water with a trunk (whelm) across and under the road into the drain passing through the close of Sir Francis Willes called Long Mead'. Two years later, in 1819, the road at Preston Hill *(shown above)* was straightened. It was thought 'narrow and dangerous'. Two local Justices of the Peace granted an order to divert the highway which involved buying small tracts of adjacent land.

They noted that over 230 yards, the road was 'for the greatest part thereof narrow and cannot be conveniently enlarged and made commodious without diverting and turning the same'. It was ruled that the road be straightened by thirty-six feet. As the maintenance of roads around Preston improved, not only did the squires travel in carriages, but several of the local tradesmen used a horse and cart. The ordinary men and women continued to regularly trudge the lanes to shop in Hitchin, visit family or get to work.

London physicians were prescribing Hitchin as a health resort. It was said that whoever 'buys a house or land in Hertfordshire pays two years purchase extraordinary for the goodness of the air'. Hence, the green lanes leading up to Preston evoked this recommendation (presumably in the summer): 'It affords a pleasant walk for the recreation of persons resident in the town (of Hitchin)'. It had a 'salubrious air, enchanting, extensive views and variety of shades'.

Yet there were still the occasional problems maintaining local lanes. In December 1892, this news story appeared: 'John Dew, farmer of Preston (*Castle Farm*) was summoned for neglecting to repair a certain highway leading from Charlton to Offley in the parish of Preston. Mr WO Times, clerk to the Hitchin Local Board, appeared for that authority. The case was brought in order that the highway (which forms the boundary of two highway districts) be divided transversely. The Bench decided that Hitchin should take the part from *Wellhead Farm* to the west corner of the Offley Holes turning, the remainder being repaired by the parish of Preston'.

Preston's pound

The nursery rhyme, *Little Boy Blue*, refers to a common predicament in village life of olden times - the problem of how to deal with stray animals and the damage they caused. The 'sheep-on-the-loose' may well be in a meadow, munching hay while a rampaging cow could run amok in the cornfield, causing swathes of damage.

A trespassing or stray animal - be it a horse, pig, cow or goose - was rounded-up and taken to the village pound by the local constable (aka *Little Boy Blue*). This was a small pen (Saxon, 'pun' - an enclosure) which was ringed by a fence or wall. The pound, probably strewn with straw and grain, was a holding cell for animals.

To release the detainee, its owner had to pay fees to the pound-keeper and the Lord of the Manor and a fine for damages. Any animals not redeemed were taken to market and sold; the proceeds being kept by the pound keeper.

Beating the Parish bounds in 2013

A similar procedure is followed today when a car is illegally parked and the police arrange for it to be towed to a (com)pound from which the vehicle can be redeemed by the payment of a fine.

The Temple Dinsley manorial records have the only historical references to Preston's pound. Even the approximate location is recorded in the roll. At a manorial court held on 22 October 1788, a note was made regarding the sale in 1770 by Edward Single of a cottage at Cranwell Green that it was '***near the pound'***, which cottage had been 'occupied by John Sharp and now Edward Andrew'. It is possible to pin-point where this cottage was *(ringed below)* - and therefore the approximate location of Preston's pound in the grounds of the present-day *Crunnells Green House* can be found:

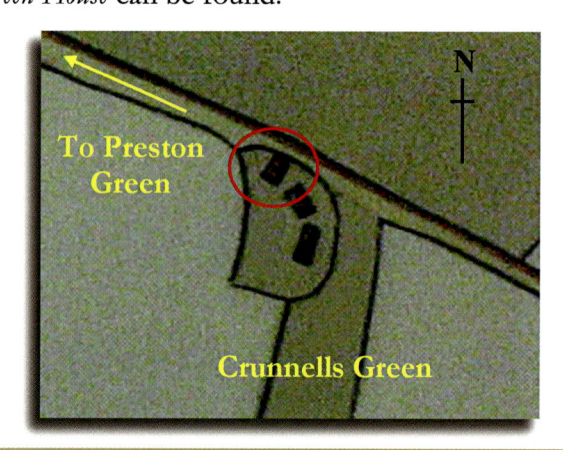

Beating the boundaries

Beating the boundaries, like the pound, was a familiar sight in Preston during the nineteenth century, yet as with references to its pound, references to the practice are rarely glimpsed in historical documents.

Parishes were not just about the tithes, upkeep and pastoral care of the local Church. Officers of the parish were also responsible for the poor, the highways and petty law and order within its perimeter. Local inhabitants grazed their livestock on common land within their parish. Hence, precisely of what land a parish consisted became more and more important.

So, through the centuries (and without maps and with a largely illiterate populace), how was the boundary of the parish remembered and its area of jurisdiction preserved?

This was no easy matter for rural parishes - especially if they were large. The boundaries were marked by immovable lines created by lanes, ditches and rivers. There were also large stones or boulders and trees which were recognised as being part of the margins.

At regular intervals, perhaps even annually, the parish priest and his officers, accompanied by local residents and children, would walk around their border to cement in several minds the knowledge of exactly where the parish ended and neighbouring parishes began. Perhaps the priest would intone a Psalm or a blessing when the markers were found. The children might beat the pivotal stones or trees with birch or willow boughs or might themselves be beaten or bumped on the markers as an extremely personal aide memoire This was known alliteratively as 'beating the bounds' or 'perambulating the parish'. The exercise could take days to complete.

There is a reference to beating the bounds around Preston in Reginald Hine's, *History of Stagenhoe*. He wrote, 'The acreage and boundaries of Earns Field Wood were certified by George Wright of *Preston Hill (Farm)* who declared himself 'well acquainted with the tenure and position of the said wood from the fact of my having acted as Overseer and having in exercise of my duties in that capacity beaten the bounds of the parish **as an annual custom**'.

Then, a document was found which describes in detail the walking of the Hitchin parish boundary during 21 - 23 May, 1801. Among the officials taking part was Joseph Darton of Temple Dinsley. Here is how the boundary around Preston was described: '....then kept the lane to Tatmore Green....kept the lane to Wayley Green and Sutfield Green....then turn to the left and inclose the whole of Mr Hinde's Further Brade (a field so called) into a lane formerly called South Lane ....continued that lane through a pond to the gate of a close (ie field) called (blank) and turned to the right inclosing the Castle, alias Hunsdon House coming straight to the cannon bank........then turn to the left down the lane (that being the boundary) to *The Chequers* signpost .... turn to the left down the road leading to Hitchin as far as the first cottage....turning to the right into a field called The Park belonging to Temple Dinsley inclosing the same to the corner of the old malting, inclosing the same to an oak pollard, the corner of Dove House Close....from thence to the north-east corner of the brick barn....from thence through the farmyard belonging to Temple Dinsley.... through a barn into the rickyard....then going by the side of the clipped hedge as far as the stile in Geddens Pasture (a field so called).. ...going thence in a direct line opposite the middle of Rase Field hedge, cross St Albans Highway ...(and returning) and the whole of Hill End Grounds to the top of Hitch Wood to St Albans Highway..... ...crossing the road into Further Bushey Field belonging to Temple Dinsley, the whole of which we inclosed and kept the foot path to the south corner of Further Burry Field.....then kept the lane leading to Preston to a cottage belonging to Mr John Gootheridge in the occupation of John Craft.... leaving the cottage on the left hand....and bearing straight to the south corner of an orchard belonging to John Princept Esq. occupied by John Brown keeping that 'til you come to the corner of a Sward Field of Mr Gootheridge, turn to the right through the hedge...... ..inclosing the whole of John Princept's land to Pains Field... then went direct across Pains Field to the rails at the corner of Long Mead.... ...inclosing the whole of Long Mead to an oak tree about 6 or 8 poles from the corner of Pains Field Wood ...from thence inclining to the right through the hedge into Long Mead and crossing the same to the spot where willow pollard formerly stood....keeping in a direct line about 2 or 3 poles to the right of the gate at the corner going into the lane (that being the spot where a cottage formerly stood), through the hedge into a field called Stockings.. ....going in a kind of angle to the west corner of the same field....through the hedge to the bottom of Dead Woman's Lane – the lane so called being the boundary to Sutfield Green as far as the gate going into Twelve Acres Sutfield belonging to *Offley Holes Farm*'.

> *George Wright of Preston Hill Farm (mid 1800s): "...having in exercise of my duties ... .beaten the bounds of the parish as an annual custom".*

This description is crammed with interesting local history information and using a detailed map from the time, it is possible to trace the exact path taken by the parish officials in 1801 (eg purple line below).

Preston's allotments

There are four historical references to the allotments at Preston. The first notes that on 22 April 1874, the Hitchin land surveyor, George Beaver (1810 - 1896), 'set out a scheme of allotment gardens in a field at Preston named "California" - the property of Henry M Pryor Esq'. This likely relates to when the allotments were created.

The sale particulars of Temple Dinsley indicates their location, the rent received from them and their area – six acres and thirty perches. The sketch map of Preston of 1884 confirms the location of the 'field gardens' and suggests how many were available to the villagers. Finally, the 'Doomsday Survey' of 1910 for the Inland Revenue mentions allotments owned by RDV Pryor and its accompanying map of 1898 shows a track or path dividing the plot.

Allotments were small areas of land set aside to allow the poor to grow vegetables and fruit. They were an important part of the villagers' life as they reduced poverty and were a source of fresh food. Some of the upper classes believed that the plots also improved morals as grafting in them kept labourers and their families from public houses and encouraged a work ethic.

But keeping an allotment was hard labour. At snatched times, after toiling in the fields and at weekends, weary men dug, sowed, weeded and harvested.

Their wives and children must have put in a substantial shift also as nature does not loiter for anyone and several crops ripened at the precise time when the allotment harvest was being gathered.

The size of each allotment can only be estimated. The 1884 sketch map shows twenty or so field gardens. However, in 1873, the annual rent received from them was £15. A typical annual rent for a plot was ten shillings (sometimes payable by instalments). If this was the arrangement in Preston, there would have been about thirty allotments. The customary size of field gardens was between 250-300 square yards - but the six acres of land (almost 30,000 square yards) set aside in Preston for allotments may indicate that the village's plots were considerably larger.

On a golden summer's night, it would have given the Pryors great satisfaction to see the villagers reaping their hard-earned harvest

To show the importance to the villagers of the allotments, in 1881 there were less than fifty households near Crunnells Green. If there were thirty plots, then about two thirds of Preston's households would have tended an allotment.

No doubt, on a golden summer's night, as the Pryors drove past in their carriage, it would have given them great satisfaction to see the villagers reaping their hard-earned harvest

The allotments were still shown on a map of Preston dated 1945.

Today, the field is uncultivated *(see below)* - perhaps the clearest sign of the change of social class of many of Preston people between the nineteenth and late twentieth centuries.

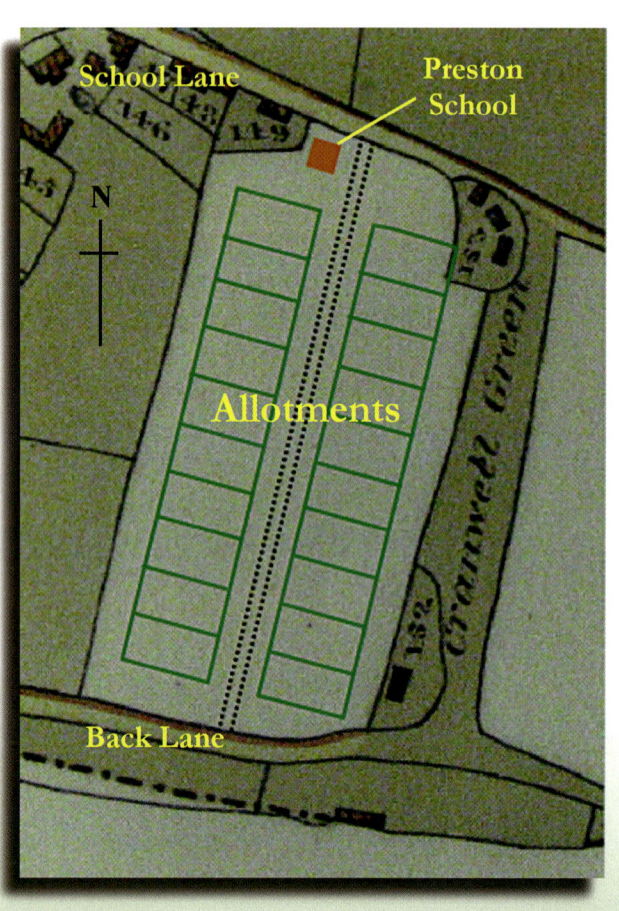

Preston's benefit clubs

Today, we are cushioned against the financial effects of illness, unemployment and old age. But in the nineteenth century, the last-resort alternatives to loss of income were the Parish Poor Law provisions and the Workhouse. Some villagers didn't mind approaching Parish officials for Poor Relief - 'They're allus a flyin' ter th' parish; they goo tew 'um at ever little tit an' turn' - but most villagers detested the thought of 'going on the parish' - 'I 'ad rather do anything 'afore I'd ask for Parish money'. And conditions within the walls of the Workhouse were hardly salubrious, being deliberately designed to deter folk from passing through its portals.

Many families at Preston were protected from financial emergencies by the earnings of plaiting wives and children. Some were fortunate enough to be able to put money aside for rainy days in Benefit Clubs. Though at Harpenden (near Preston), Edwin Grey commented 'I could hardly see how it was possible for them to save anything from their small wage' - until he saw 'that nearly all the thrifty ones were men with only one or two children or no family at all' and those who were 'not given to excessive drinking'.

These clubs were formed in the first half of the nineteenth century (the earliest reference to one at Preston is in 1837) by labourers who collected their peers' savings regularly and paid sick, aged and unemployed members of clubs from the accumulated funds. How else were labourers to store their little hoards? Walking to Hitchin to make deposits in banks took time and energy. If they stashed it about their hovels, there was the risk of fire or theft. Also, as the insurance industry well knows, there is protection in numbers - labourers bandied together could look after each other's interests. Clubs were able to negotiate discounts for clothing and coal due to bulk-buying for their members. The comparatively better off - the rate-payers - welcomed this thriftiness by the herd. There were less demands on Parish Poor Relief and so their own onerous contributions were reduced.

The club was held at *The Chequers* inn. On Saturday, 7 January 1837, John Ward, assaulted John Squires as he came out of the door of *The Chequers* 'where his club had been held that evening'. It was as well that the disturbance was not within the public house - as well as the 15/- fine that Ward incurred, he might have forfeited a further 10/- to the club according to its rules! As well as the monthly meetings, each year it is likely that there was an annual feast day at *The Chequers*.

This is inferred as there were reported feast days at Kings Walden and it is unlikely that Preston villagers would have allowed their neighbours and bitter rivals to have *all* the fun. Feast days were 'the fete of the labourer' when there was plenty to eat and drink with singing, dancing and laughter. They were usually held around Whitsun - in May 1845, Francis Sharpe of Preston, was charged with assaulting John Buck, inn-keeper of the *Frogmore Fox Inn*, Kings Walden. Sharpe and others went to the pub 'on a day when the club feast was held there and called for beer'. When this was refused, he assaulted Buck and threatened to put in his windows.

Two Preston school children provide an insight into other clubs that served the village by 1910. One wrote of an imaginary Mrs Tidy, 'I pay into the coal club, so at Christmas I have it out and I have enough to last me through the winter and there is Mrs Untidy shivering with cold just because she won't pay into the club and there is her husband at the public house spending all his money'. Another girl wrote as the fictional Mrs Tidy, 'My husband gets £1 a week and I spend 4/- for rent, 1/- for the coal club and 3/- for the clothing club. Then I also put 9d by each week in case of illness and the other 10/- I have to use for food'. Whether these amounts are accurate is a moot point, but the comments give an indication of what clubs were in the village and the contributions made by their members.

Coal club members saved a weekly small amount and collectively were able to negotiate a discount with coal merchants. Within the club, widows and the infirm were given preferential benefits and occupants of cottages with low rateable values could buy coal at wholesale prices and receive interest on deposits. The Clothing Club operated in the same way as the Coal Club. The Preston School log book records that on 10 December 1901, seventeen children were 'absent in afternoon owing to children going to Hitchin to buy clothes with club cards'. A relative recalls that Hawkins of Hitchin was one of the draper's shops used by Preston Club. '(It was) of much benefit to cottagers, great consultations being held when the Club cards came out as to what material, household linen, or coat or suit could be procured for the amount of money deposited.

Preston's Club Reading Room was built after 1879 - perhaps it was erected by the Pryors. It was home to newspapers and hundreds of books and was built to promote community knowledge and learning. The clapboard building on the Kings Walden Road beside *The Old Forge*, still stands today *(see page 60)*.

Cricket

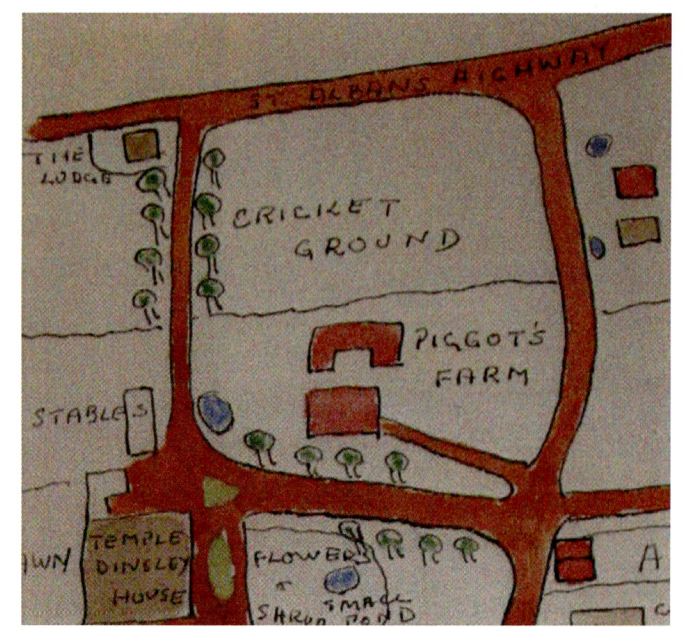

There has been a tradition of cricket at Preston since at least 1884, when the sketch map *(right)* was made. The earliest report seen of a Preston cricket match was in 1911. By this time, matches were being played in the Park of Temple Dinsley (now Princess Helena College). The marquee and pitch were located by the St Albans Highway drive and 'near to where the magnificent horse-chestnut trees now stand'.

D Frost wrote, 'It would seem…that the team would largely consist of either sons or guests or friends from the Estate, with the addition of one or two Estate workers, and one or two independents from the village. There would be little time in those days for farm workers to play (the combine harvester was yet to come) and their hours would be fully occupied throughout the summer months with haymaking, harvesting etc. Sundays were, of course, for them a day of leisure, a day to wear their best, and probably only suit, and a day to seek out and talk to friends and acquaintances.

'Some derelict farm buildings stood on the land now occupied by the houses (on the north side of Chequers Lane and these rude sheds were to be the first 'pavilion' when cricket started in 1919. Douglas Vickers at Temple Dinsley gave permission for the meadows to be used as a cricket ground. The outfield was only cut for haymaking.

'(After the Great War) the two Pryors (Geoffrey and Ralston) with Reginald Dawson (the estate agent) were the driving forces in the reformation of the club, and they were playing members when the team was captained by Lord Scott. Other members of this team were Jack Flint (estate carpenter), Fred Longley (who looked after the domestic engines of the Estate), Hubert Peters and Bob Wray.

Preston C.C. 1923 - *Standing (l to r)*: Robert Wray, J Murphy, J Garner, GIE Pryor, PC.Dear, R Chapman *(umpire)*. *Middle row (l to r)*: Frank Wray, R Dawson, C Darton, F Longley. *Front row (l to r)*: Rev. Stainsbury, W Peters *(scorer)*, S Chapman.

'In 1921, the Pavilion was built, the bricks and tiles for it being made in a shed on Brown's Farm, and the woodwork prepared by Jack Flint at Kiln Wood. An enclosure was erected in front of the Pavilion for the exclusive use of members and ladies. A tennis court was also established here. Both an Evangelical Tented Mission and a Fair were permitted to use the ground and during the war years the Army used the ground. It has also been host to Jubilee and Coronation celebrations and the Annual Fete and Flower Show.'

'The Recreation Ground as we now know it was part of the farmland of Brown's Farm. On the death of the farmer in 1912/13 the property and attached land passed into the ownership of the Estate. A sparse hedge ran from roughly where the old pavilion now stands in a direct line to the Hitchin Road and a number of elm and oak trees stood at various points in these two meadows.

Preston - best-kept, smaller Herts. village, 1959

Preston had entered the competition in previous years without success and the feeling was that the village should not be entered again. However, the benefits of taking part were appealing - the resulting improvement in the appearance of the village, the integration of the community and the improved spirit it would produce. The Head Mistress of Princess Helena College generously co-operated by making her girls responsible for the removal of all the debris and litter – 'they made a fine contribution'. Many other volunteers came forward and with machinery borrowed from a local farmer, hedges were trimmed, ditches were cleaned and hedgerows cut with an Allen cutter. Villagers could be seen working hard every evening until dusk.

Preston had a thriving Horticultural Society and their members organised improvements to the village's gardens, supplied flowering shrubs and gave advice. A number of trees were also planted. That year, Preston won the cherished competition – and won it again the following year! An awards ceremony was held on The Green and the presentation was made by the Hon. David Bowes Lyon *(above, right)*.

Hertfordshire Countryside reported that, 'Now the grass is kept like a lawn and the charm of the village can be appreciated...the well-kept hedges add to the beauty of the village centre...a few years ago the centre of Preston was untidy and unkempt with the grass long and the verges, ragged... Preston was the most improved village (though it) lost points as there were no seats on the seats in the recreation ground.'

A transformation from that............to this

Preston Green

Historically, an annual sheep fair was held at The Green. It was criss-crossed by wide paths which were said to be sheep tracks. These are plainly seen from the sketch map dated 1884 shown right. By 1873, the Green had become the location for a travelling fun fair which was held at the end of September. The village children saved their pennies from collecting acorns (which were fed to pigs) to enjoy the delights of the rides and the stalls. Unsurprisingly, the school log entry for 28 September 1885 reads, "attendance very low owing to a fair being held on the green".

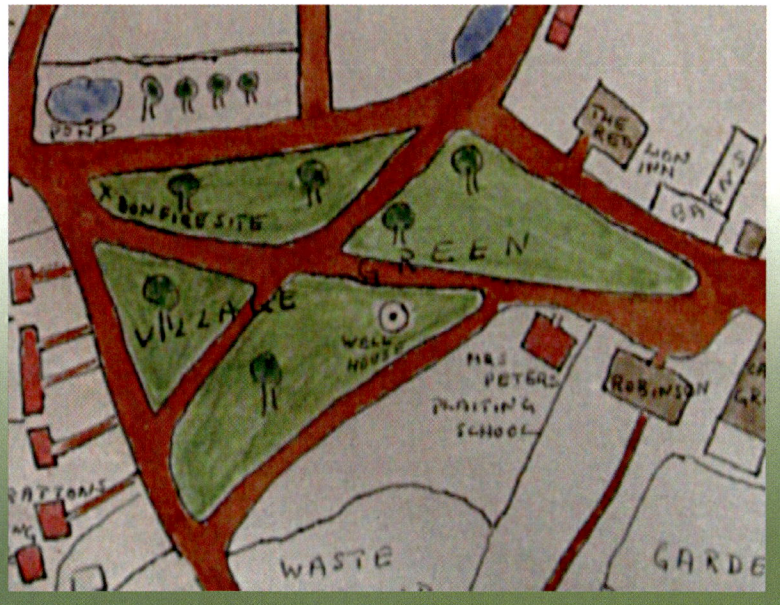

Preston Green *continued*

During the evening of the fair on The Green, the fun continued as there was dancing at the *Red Lion*. Sometimes, a fiddler was hired to provide the music. Admission to the dance room cost 2d. The fair was last held in 1914. Another attraction on the Green was the annual bonfire - the site of which is marked on the map.

The Green has been the natural place of assembly for large gatherings of villagers - from overflow meetings at Bunyan's Chapel to hog roasts celebrating the community buy-out of the *Red Lion*.

For centuries, the Green had been dominated by five elms, as shown above. The elms were planted in 1761 and commemorated the coronation of King George III. Nearly two hundred years later, the saplings had grown into giants and a report noted that some were in a dangerous condition - although, it was added, there was no need for them to be felled. Representatives of the deceased owner of The Green, Mr Barrington-White, debated the future of the elms with Hitchin Rural District Council.

In January 1946, the County Surveyor wrote that he was not aware of any suggestion that the trees should be felled – but before his letter was delivered, the first elm had been cut down. Despite efforts to halt the destruction of the four remaining trees, they too were felled. The aftermath is pictured below.

A consequence of this unsatisfactory situation was that Preston Green (together with land at Crunnells Green and the verge between the eastern boundary of Temple Dinsley and St Albans Highway) was purchased by the village for £5 which was raised by public subscription. After consulting the Conservator of the Forests of the City of London, lime and thorn trees were planted to replace the elms. For the coronation of another monarch, Elizabeth II, in 1953, another tree was planted at Preston Green – an oak. The sapling had sprouted from an acorn taken from the tree at Hatfield Park under which Elizabeth I had been sitting when she heard news that she had acceeded to the throne. The young tree was planted by the oldest Preston resident, Herbert Sharp (88) *(shown below)* and one of the youngest boys, William Stanley *(3, the boy on the extreme left)*.

Above are two views of The Green in the 1950s after the elms had been replaced. The photograph on the right was taken in 2008. By now many of the wide 'tracks' had been filled in and grassed.

The well at Preston Green

The well at Preston Green is an historic, iconic symbol of village life - it appears on today's Preston Parish newsletter and is featured on the title page of the *Preston Scrapbook*. Yet events leading up to its sinking may be misunderstood.

The *Scrapbook* states: 'The Well on the Green was the gift of William Henry Darton….It was dug in the hot dry summer of 1872 when most of the ponds had dried up'. This may well be true, but a document that has recently come to light paints a different picture.

In 1870, Mr Weeks was living at Temple Dinsley. On 12 October 1870, he felt constrained to write the following letter to William H Darton: 'I have observed with deep regret that my poorer neighbours in the village of Preston have no water fit to drink and medical gentlemen of the district have certified to me that a large amount of illness results from the unwholesome and filthy water which the cottagers are compelled to use. I, with many other residents in the neighbourhood, consider it a duty we owe to those who cannot assist themselves to use our utmost endeavours to procure such a supply of pure water as is necessary to preserve the life and health of the inhabitants. I therefore beg to solicit your co-operation in this desirable undertaking by giving permission for the opening of ground on Preston Green on which to sink a deep well and also granting a convenient place where the excavated soil may be deposited.' Thus, although Darton may have allowed and financed the sinking of the well, the prime mover in its construction was Mr Weeks.

When sunk, the well was 211' 8" deep. Two people operated the winding mechanism and they toiled for five minutes to raise the water. A villager remembers, 'collecting water from the village pump on the green, even after mains water was piped to the houses, because people were suspicious of piped water'.

There is an octagonal well house open at the sides with a steep-pointed octagonal slate roof and eight chamfered stout oak posts which are raised on concrete pads. The cast-iron well gear is arranged over the top of the well. It consists of an rectangular, openwork, moulded iron trestle with battered ends. It has two four-feet-wide diameter flywheels with handles, one at each end of lower axle. A cog of fifteen teeth engages a gear of ninety-six teeth on the upper axle, which also carries a flanged iron drawing pulley. There is a larger gear of sixty teeth on the lower axle. The roof is fashioned from softwood. The well was disused and fenced off by 1930.

At various times there were also wells at *Castle Farm, Pond Farm*, Austage End, *Preston Hill Farm, The Wilderness* at Butchers Lane and Temple Dinsley.

(Top) The well in the 1930s; *(those below)* in 2008

The historic cottages of Preston

Preston Green: *Kenwood Cottage, Club House* and *Joyner's Cottage*

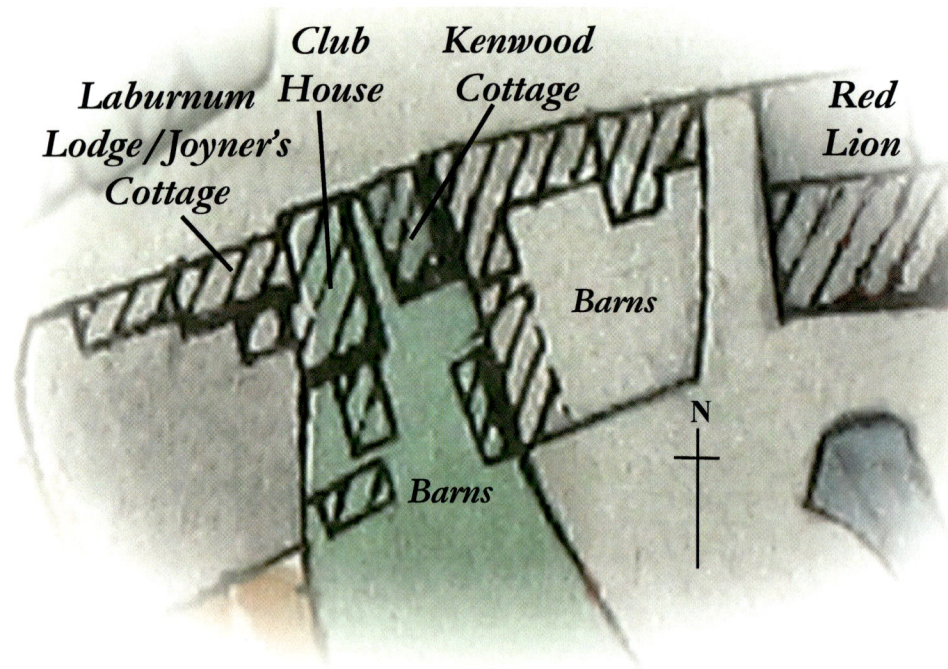

Laburnum Lodge/Joyner's Cottage — *Club House* — *Kenwood Cottage* — *Red Lion* — Barns — Barns — N

By 1884, a weather-boarded barn had been added to the west end of *Laburnum Lodge* cottage *(see bottom, left)* which was not described in sales particulars dated 1873.

In the 1880s, The *Lodge* was the village post office. Soon after 1910, the barn was demolished and a new cottage added to the west end of *Laburnum Lodge* - as can be seen from the photograph shown immediately below.

For at least the last six decades, *The Club House* and *Laburnum Lodge* have existed as one property - a survey in 1973 noted, of *Laburnum Lodge*, 'including C19 cottage adjoining to the west, all now one cottage'.

Kenwood Cottage was built in the middle of the nineteenth century, probably by the Dartons. It is a two-storey cottage constructed in red brickwork with a hipped slate roof. In 1910, it comprised a living room, kitchen, scullery and two bedrooms. It had a wood and slated barn. It was owned by H Fenwick of Temple Dinsley and was in 'good repair'.

It is difficult to determine precisely when *The Club House* and its neighbour *Laburnum Lodge (now Joyners Cottage)* were built. A survey in 1973 recorded that they were both constructed in the seventeenth century. The two homes are not recorded in the 1664 Survey of Temple Dinsley but *are* mentioned in a survey of 1714. Thus, the manorial record suggests that the two homes were built between those dates.

c. 1913

c. 1890

2008

58

Pryor House aka *The Laburnums*

The Laburnums (right) was built by Ralston de Vins Pryor in the 1890s. In 1910, it was noted as a 'brick and tiled house with a drawing room, dining room, kitchen, scullery, laundry room and wc on the ground floor and a bathroom and four bedrooms on the first floor. In around 1956, its residents were Stewart and Rosemary McConville who likely re-christened it, *Pryor House*.

Fig Tree, Vine and Peters' Cottages

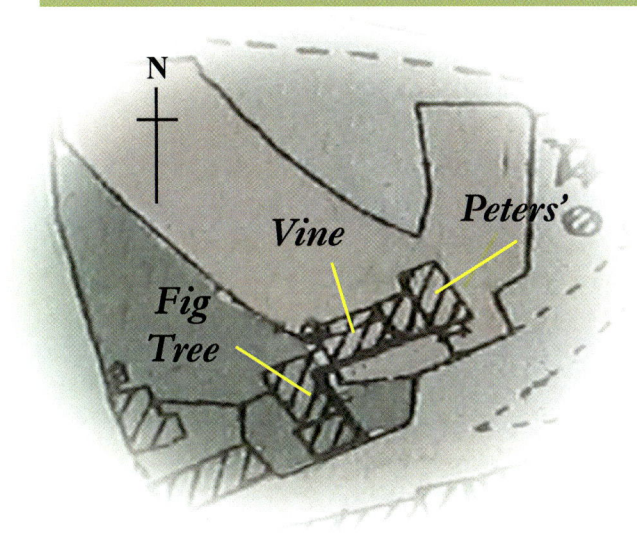

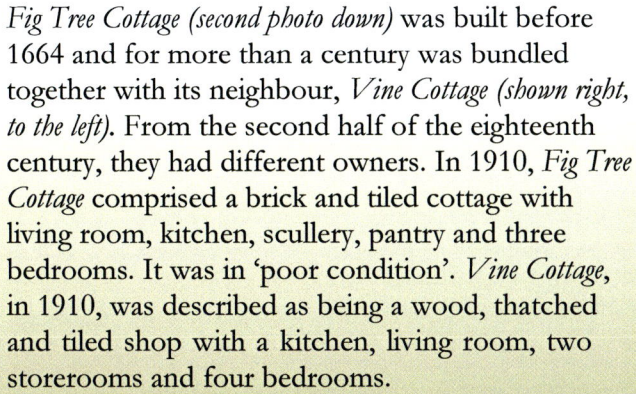

Fig Tree Cottage *(second photo down)* was built before 1664 and for more than a century was bundled together with its neighbour, *Vine Cottage (shown right, to the left)*. From the second half of the eighteenth century, they had different owners. In 1910, *Fig Tree Cottage* comprised a brick and tiled cottage with living room, kitchen, scullery, pantry and three bedrooms. It was in 'poor condition'. *Vine Cottage*, in 1910, was described as being a wood, thatched and tiled shop with a kitchen, living room, two storerooms and four bedrooms.

The carpenter's shop, *(third photo down, far right)* was first referred to as a home occupied by Joseph Peters in 1825 - hence I am referring to it as *Peters' Cottage*. As described earlier, Sarah Peters ran a plaiting school from this property. However, it is possible that this building was inhabited *before* 1825. From 1797, the run of entries in rates books indicate that there was a home here at the end of the eighteenth century. By 1898, *Peters' Cottage* was Frederick Robinson's tailor's shop. Eventually it was demolished and a new village shop was built in its place which traded well into the twentieth century.

Cottages at Church Lane

The Old Forge

Shown right is a cluster of buildings shown on a map dated 1898 including *The Old Forge* (circled). There is a note that the house was built in the early C18 and that shortly after it was built, the property had some additions: 'A south-west wing and formerly separate east wing (were added) a few years later'. This is confirmed by the Temple Dinsley Manorial Records. The first mention of this property was probably in 1713. By 1881, the house had been divided into two dwellings of four rooms each. The bake-house and baker's home was on the west side. In 1910, cottage 1 was of brick and tile construction and had a kitchen and two bedrooms. It was in poor repair. Cottage 2 was also of brick and tile and contained a bake-house, living room and kitchen. It was in poor repair. Attached to the building was a wood and thatched stable and a barn. Moving into the twentieth century, the blacksmith's shop had been demolished and in its place stood the Preston Club Reading Room *(shown top right)*.

St Martin's Place

It has been said that *St Martin's Place* was built in the seventeenth century or earlier and that the front wall of the house was constructed in around 1700. Another survey in 1973 concluded that it was built in the eighteenth century. The first firm historical references to it are in the Hitchin Rates Books from 1801 to 1811

In 1910, the house was described as a red brick cottage and shop with a living room, kitchen, pantry and four bedrooms. It was in poor repair.

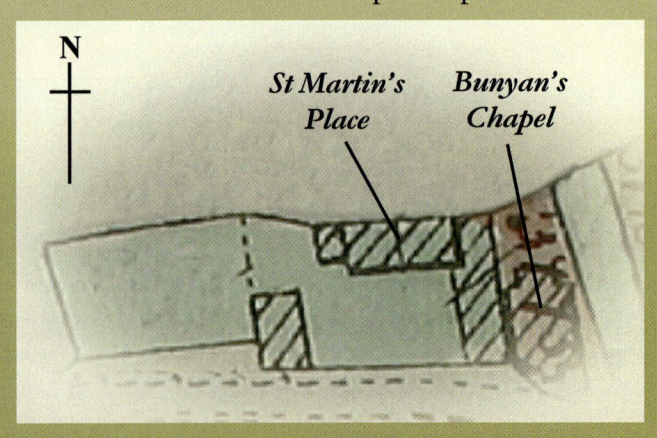

Cottages to the east of *Bunyan's Chapel*

Both cottages immediately to the east of *Bunyan's Chapel* were built before 1664. In 1920, Cottage **A** *(shown, right)* was described as 'brick and thatched with a kitchen, pantry and two bedrooms...in poor repair'. Cottage **B** *(shown, second down)* was known as *Gentle's Cottage*. In 1910, it was 'brick and tiled with a kitchen, washroom and two bedrooms'. It was 'a little cottage which faced the side of the *Bunyan Chapel*. The cottage was of clapboard construction and had a barn attached to one side, with a bedroom built over the barn'. Both cottages were demolished before 1938.

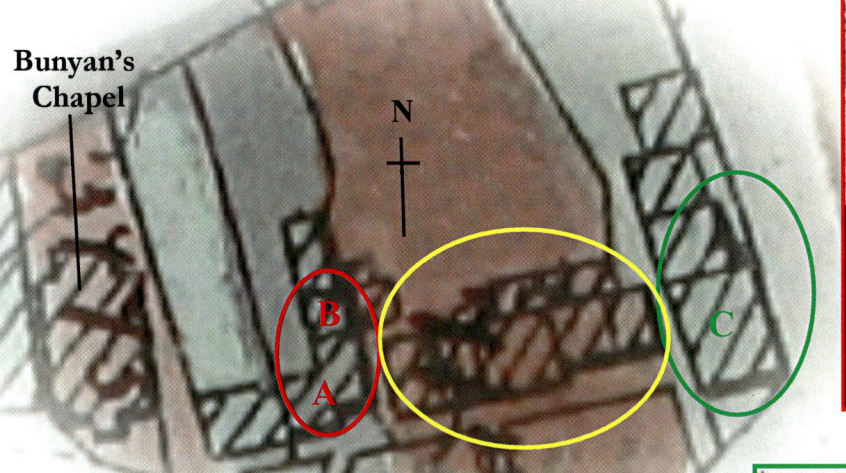

A c. 1930

B c. 1920

The cottages to the Hitchin Road

There were two adjoining cottages on the corner with the Hitchin Road *(circled green)*. The home to the south (**C**) was built before 1664 and in 1910 was described as a brick and tiled cottage with a kitchen and two bedrooms. The property to the north, *Line's Cottage*, was probably built in the 1690s and in 1910 was of brick and tiles, having a kitchen and two bedrooms. Both properties were demolished between 1913 and 1937 - that is, before the other adjacent cottages along Church Lane (below) were knocked down.

C c.1913

There was a row of three cottages to the east of cottage **A** which were built in around 1810. These were attached to two homes which were built before 1662, (see next page) which were to the east. All five cottages *(circled yellow)* consisted of a kitchen and two bedrooms. They had all been demolished by 1938.

c. 1913

c. 1913

(Above) A charming view of the cottages on the corner of Church Lane and Hitchin Road. The seven cottages along Church Lane that were featured on the previous page were replaced by *Preston House (right)* which was built and designed by Alfred D Allington in 1938.

2008

Cottages on School Lane

Red Lion

School Lane

1

2 & 3

4

N

2008

Cottage **1** was built before 1664; Cottages **2/3**, in the 1690s. When cottage **4** was erected is unclear. Early in the nineteenth century, cottage **1** was converted into three homes. All six homes comprised a kitchen and one bedroom with one exception which boasted two bedrooms. These homes were demolished in 1919 by Douglas Vickers. Four bungalows were erected in their place in 1920 *(middle right)*. One is now the Preston Village Hall.

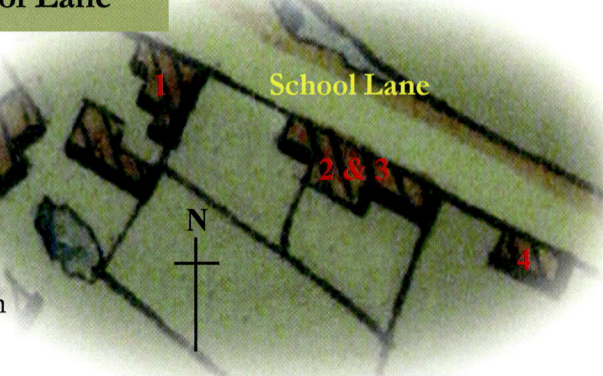

c. 1913

Cottages at Crunnells Green

Both cottages were constructed before 1664. At some point the one to the south-west was temporarily converted into two homes. They were both described as being of brick and tile with a kitchen, pantry, two bedrooms and a garden.

They were demolished by Herbert Fenwick in around 1908. In 1919, Crunnells Green House (which has been previously shown) replaced them majestically.

c. 1913

c. 1913

Cottages at Wright's/Armstrong's Lane

At the beginning of the nineteenth century, there were at least four cottages along the road that leads from Back Lane to *Preston Hill Farm*. All but one were demolished between 1871 and 1881.

On the map shown above from 1848, the four cottages are circled with *Reeves Cottage* ringed in red.

The one remaining home, *Preston Hill Farm Cottage* aka *Reeves Cottage*, is shown right. It is said to be 'late medieval' (i.e. built in the sixteenth century).

2010

Cottages at Back Lane

There were ten tumbledown cottages along Back Lane at the beginning of the twentieth century which were built between 1664 - 1674 *(right)*. Most consisted of just two rooms in total but three homes were 'two-up; two down'.

Apart from two semi-detached homes which were built of brick and had thatched roofs, the others were all brick-built with tiled roofs. These homes were demolished in around 1916.

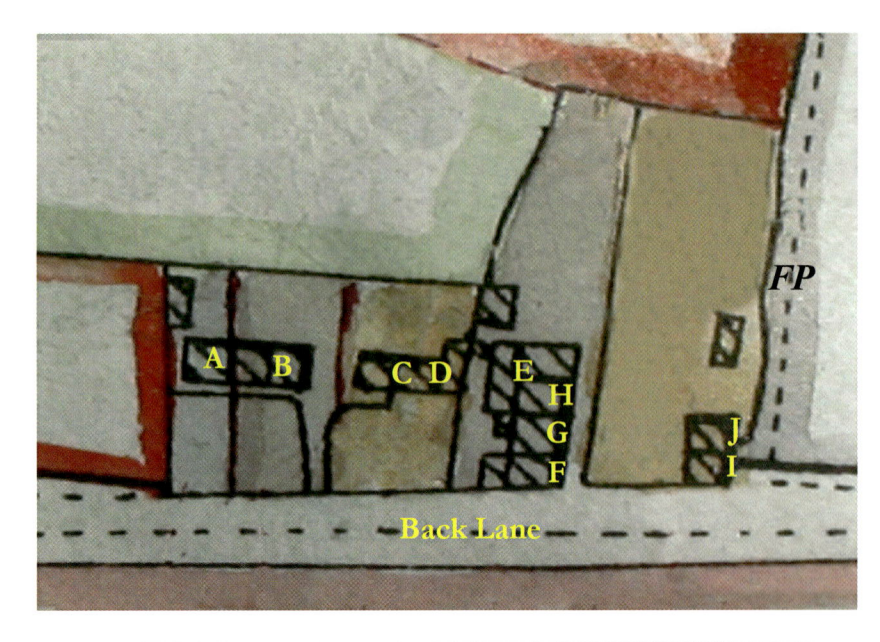

Spindle Cottage

Spindle Cottage, Hitchin Road, has a plaque stating it was built in 1717. It was Preston's Post Office for around 40 years until 1939. A burglary was committed here on a Saturday night in December 1904. Mrs Frost (70) and her daughter screamed when they found two men in the house. They demanded a sovereign each as their families were starving. After taking a half sovereign and some coppers they shook hands with Mrs Frost and her daughter and left.

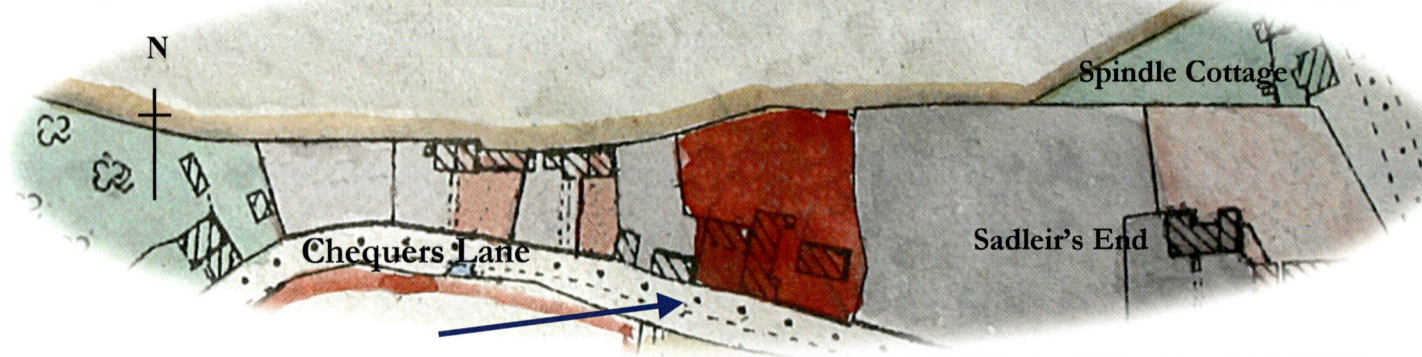

Cottages at Chequers Lane

There were around eleven houses on the north side of Chequers Lane in the nineteenth century, including the inn. With the exception of *The Chequers* and *Sadleir's End* it is impossible to say when these houses were built. From a description in 1910, it is clear that many of these old, tumbledown cottages were 'in poor order' and were soon to be demolished. There were probably only four homes inhabited here in 1920, so it is likely that the process of razing them and building new council houses had started by then. The photograph on the right was taken in the direction of the blue arrow on the map.

Sadleir's End, Chequers Lane

Although *Sadleir's End* has '1719' inscribed above its front door, it was built early in the sixteenth century. In 1910, it was described as a brick and tiled house. It comprised of a sitting room, kitchen, scullery, pantry and three bedrooms. On its land was a wood and corrugated iron stable.

The junction of Chequers Lane and Butchers Lane

This rather remote corner of Preston was populated by three homes in the nineteenth century - though one was demolished in the late 1880s. Though isolated, it was busy - at various times a tailor, a butcher and a wheelwright plied their trade there. *Rose Cottage (right)* has an eighteenth century exterior, but was probably built earlier. *The Wilderness* was erected in the early eighteenth century. In 1910, both had a living room, kitchen, scullery and three bedrooms. *Rose Cottage* also had two attics.

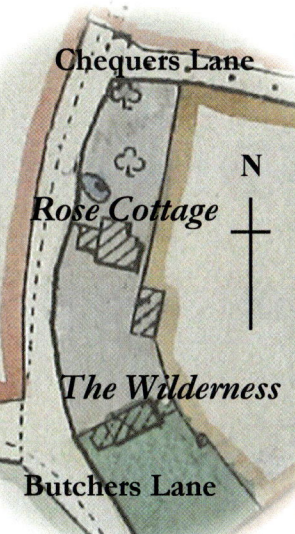

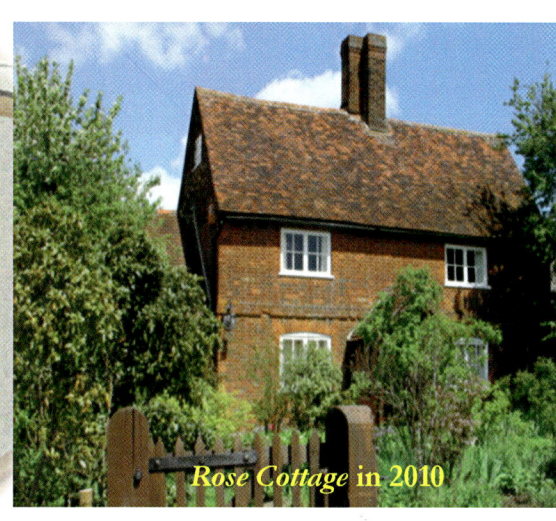

Rose Cottage in 2010

The Wilderness in 2010

Sootfield Green, Charlton Road

Sootfield (or Southfield) Green is a mile north-west of Preston Green. The Hertfordshire Archaeological Trust states 'evidence of medieval and post medieval settlement (here) is indicated by the remains of former buildings'. The two cottages at Sootfield Green were erected in the eighteenth century and were 'two-up; two-down' homes. Probably in the 1920s, they were converted into one dwelling.

Sootfield Green was in Hitchen parish, although it was squeezed to the west by Kings Walden and to the east by Ippollitts.

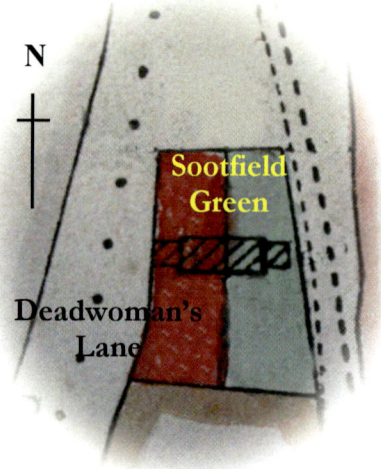

Estate Cottages at Preston

To provide accommodation for their present and previous workers, the estates of Temple Dinsley and Kings Walden Bury built two rows of cottages at Preston. They both had sizeable gardens and brick barns to support their residents' gardening activities.

1-6 Chequers Cottages, Chequers Lane *(right)* were designed by Sir Edwin Lutyens and financed by HG Fenwick of Temple Dinsley in 1914 to replace the insanitary cottages in the village which had been demolished. The homes in the middle section had a kitchen, a scullery, a living room and three bedrooms.

Holly Cottages (right), Back Lane, were so named because of the holly bushes which fronted them and were built by September 1918. They had a kitchen/dining room with a fireplace and a walk-in pantry, together with a coal/wood cellar. Upstairs were two bedrooms, front and back. There was also a small box room on this floor that was large enough for another wardrobe and perhaps a child's crib.

Offley Holes Farm

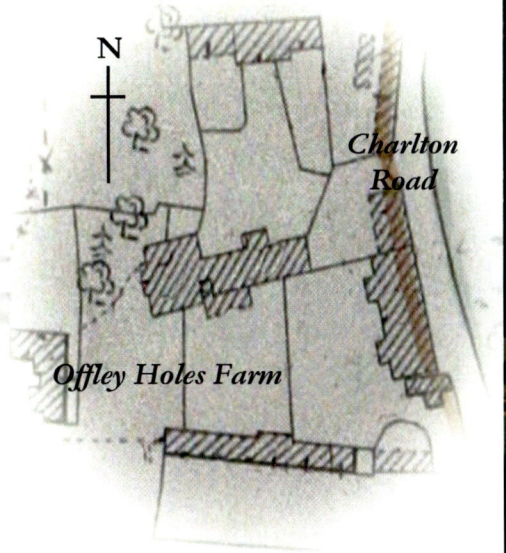

The first reference found that relates to *Offley Holes Farm* is by JEB Glover in *Place Names of Hertfordshire*. He asserts that a document at Trinity College, Cambridge (dated 1650) mentioning 'Offleyholes' is a reference to the farm. The existence of a farm at Offley Holes is confirmed by a run of documents from 1654 to 1701 when Sir Edwin Sadleir, Lord of the Manor of Temple Dinsley, sought to confirm his title to the 'capital messuage (that is, main dwelling) or farm house called Offley Holes' and its associated land. North Herts. DC estimates that *Offley Holes Farm* was built in 1700. Today's owner was told that the present building was erected in around 1710. Yet, as described above, there was a farm at Offley Holes in the 1650s, so it was demolished and replaced or modified early in the eighteenth century.

Offley Holes House

Offley Holes Farm was owned by the Curling family for most of the nineteenth century. Robert Curling died in 1894. In his will he issued instructions that 'a sum not exceeding £4,000 should be spent erecting a residence...upon my estate in Hertfordshire'. The house was built 'so high up the hill that a pump house had to be built in the farmyard at its foot'. This building still stands *(above left)*. The mansion *(right)* was leased out until, on 28 January 1918, the War Office took possession of the house. It was earmarked as a camp for German prisoners of war. The building was completely destroyed by fire on 12 February 1919. Villagers believed this was caused by a 'foul chimney'. Nothing remains of the House now but a few bits of masonry and garden flowers. There was still the thorny legal question of liability and compensation. After a lengthy battle in the courts the previous tenant, Percy St Clair Matthey, was found to be liable for the cost of reconstruction. But the house was never rebuilt.

The Dower House aka The Cottage, Hitchin Road

In the eighteenth century, *Preston Farm* was based at the property known today as *The Dower House*. The research trail begins with the manorial records of Maidencroft.

They note in 1742, that there was a farm with a house known as *Barons* and that a later owner sold the holding to Joseph Darton of Temple Dinsley on 11 November 1800.

In 1818, Ippollitts parish was enclosed and the map and the document that accompanied it showed where Preston Farm and most of its fields were situated.

North Herts. District Council when surveying Preston noted that *The Dower House* dated from the early eighteenth century.

c. 1913

c. 1913

2008

2008

Elizabeth Darton was living at *The Cottage* in 1851 and her son, Thomas Darton, was there in 1871. *The Cottage*, as it was now known, was part of the estate when Temple Dinsley was sold to the Pryors in 1873. The hyperbole of the selling agents included these descriptions: 'pleasantly situated', 'charming and secluded', 'a bijou residence' (or, small but elegant and tasteful), and 'Shooting Box' (or, a small country house used by hunters in season). It comprised a dining room, drawing room, library, kitchen, scullery, cellar, dairy, eight bedrooms, two dressing rooms, an attic and w.c. Attached were stables, coach house and a small farm yard together with green and hot houses in the garden.

There was also a private walk through a shrubbery to the village which emerged by the rail pond at Preston Green. In 1910, *The Cottage* had been sub-divided into two gardener's cottages. The first consisted of a hall, sitting room, kitchen, scullery, larder, three bedrooms, a box-room, bathroom and w.c. The second cottage had a living room, sitting room, kitchen, three bedrooms, bothy and a scullery. The outbuildings included a boot-house, two coach-houses, a harness room, two bedrooms, two w.cs., two wood and corrugated iron loose boxes, a wood and tiled stables for four horses with stove and loft and a greenhouse. Today, *The Dower House (above)* is part of Princess Helena College.

Castle Farm

To the north of Chequers Lane, a mansion, *Hunsdon House*, was built near the site of Preston Castle. Nearby was a well which was 270 feet deep. In the 1660s, *Hunsdon House* at Preston was home to the Foster brothers – six of them (three married, three bachelors) lived there. They were 'intimate friends and enthusiastic followers' of John Bunyan, offering the preacher a welcome and shelter in their home during troublesome times. The Fosters sold *Hunsdon House* and its farmland to Joseph Roberts who, in 1723, sold the property and land to Robert Hinde *(see page 22)*.

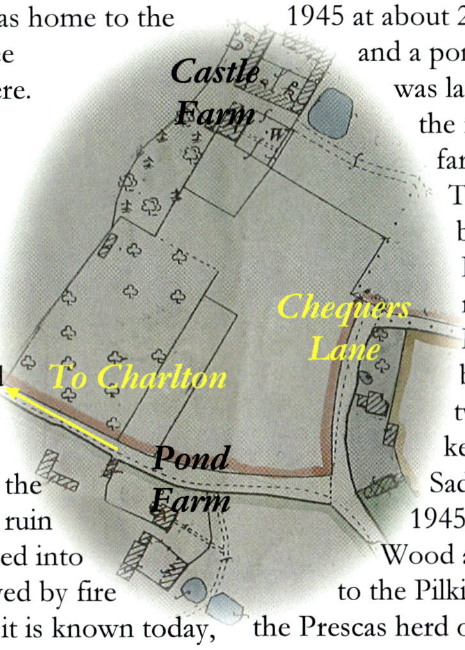

Hunsdon House fell into disrepair in the early nineteenth century and was a ruin by the 1850s. A stable was converted into a farmhouse – but this was destroyed by fire in 1868. *Castle Farm (above right)*, as it is known today, was then built. A house at the junction with Chequers Lane was added later *(above left)*.

The area of farmland (which is both arable and pasture) associated with *Hunsdon House* and *Castle Farm* was remarkably unchanged between 1861 and 1945 at about 278 acres. It included a chalk pit and a pond to the north of the farm that was large enough to provide water when the fire brigade attempted to save the farmhouse and buildings in 1868. The land was divided by the parish boundaries of Hitchin and Ippollitts and fell within the manors of Temple Dinsley and Maidencroft. The farmland bordered Wain Wood. In the twentieth century, Douglas Vickers kept a famous herd of Wessex Saddleback pigs at *Castle Farm*. In 1945, the farm, together with Wain Wood and its surrounding fields, was sold to the Pilkington Estate. It has been home to the Prescas herd of pedigree Holstein Fresian cows.

Pond Farm

Pond Farm (shown right) occupied a compact block of land south from the farmhouse, along Butchers Lane and along the Kings Walden Road, between Butchers Lane and Dead Woman's Lane. In the eighteenth century, the families of Turner, Simmes, Godfrey and Hill were associated with the farm. *Pond Farm* was sold in 1884. The sales particulars well describe the farm, where a new house had recently been built. The farm land consisted of old pasture and market garden land of forty acres which was 'considered to be some of the best land in the neighbourhood' with perfect drainage due to the nature of the soil. There were ponds of water on the property - hence the farm's name, presumably.

The ponds included one which was fed by a spring that had never been known to fail. The estate was sold for £1,375 to John Harvey Lovell of Brighton and George Bryan Milman from London. They owned a well-arranged and substantially-built farm which had been recently erected. It had a cattle yard partially enclosed by brick wall; a brick-built and slated open cattle shed; a stable for four horses; a chaff house; a loose box or piggery; a three-bayed open cart shed; a granary and a hen house. Nearby were two brick, timber and thatched buildings - a cow house and a corn barn.

Preston Hill Farm

At the beginning of the nineteenth century, *Preston Hill Farm* was owned by John Gootheridge (c.1770 -1850). The Goothridges had lived in Preston and farmed at *Preston Hill* for centuries. The farm grew from 227 acres in 1816 to 246 acres in 1848 and 1885. It farmed the block of land between Back Lane/Wright's Lane and the road to Whitwell. Some of the names of its fields changed during the nineteenth century. In 1816 there were *Great* and *Little Goslingdell*, *Elmer's Orchard* and *Foxholes*. By 1885, new field names had been coined: *Reeves Meadow*, *May's Meadow* and *Ward's Meadow*. A comparison of historic maps and awards shows that many of the fields of 1848 had been amalgamated into larger tracts of land by 1885. The hedgerows clearly portrayed in 1848 had been uprooted as the fields expanded. It was evidently felt that several fields were too small for efficient farming. Possibly also the hedgerows were preventing the uniform ripening of crops.

John Goothridge died in 1850. Shortly before his death, he sold *Preston Hill Farm*. The sale particulars provide a wonderful description of the farm: The main farmhouse had six bedrooms, a kitchen, two parlours or sitting rooms, a brew-house, washhouse and two beer and wine cellars. The outbuildings included six corn barns (five with planking, one with clinkers), stabling, a two-storey granary and two 'warm cattle yards'. It was 'a compact and truly desirable enclosed farm' of 240 acres of arable land, pasture and woodland. John Goothridge had followed a succession of corn, turnips and clover.

There were three cattle ponds and a 'well of never failing pure water'. The surrounding area was extolled as 'abounding with game and in the vicinity of foxhounds'. The farm included four cottages to house its labourers. Following its sale, *Preston Hill Farm* became part of the Kings Walden Estate and was managed from 1850 until the 1870s by George Wright. After his death, the farm was run by Frederick Armstrong. Around this time, a new farmhouse was built *(shown above)*. 'Freddie' Maybrick farmed here during the first half of the twentieth century. Today, *Preston Hill Farm* is a cattery.

Home Farm

The *Home Farm* farmstead was situated on the west side of the Hitchin Road, Preston opposite *The Cottage (Dower House)* and just north of the present-day Preston Cricket Ground. It was in the parish of Ippollitts. From 1788 it was owned by Sir Francis Willes and thence Francis Lovell. A few years after Lovell's death, in August 1906, his holding was absorbed into the Temple Dinsley estate.

The 1861 census notes that the farm occupied 140 acres. This assessment is confirmed by a schedule which shows *Home Farm* consisting of 133 acres within three parishes: Ippollitts (60 acres), Hitchin (27) and Kings Walden (26). Indeed this farm sprawled over more than 1½ miles with islands of fields dotted here and there. The farm out-buildings were part of the Minsden Estate in 1945 and were sold as 'the Estate Yard' in a lot together with *Castle Farm* and Wain Wood. The farmhouse gradually became derelict and by 1967 a Herts. C.C. Highways Department yard occupied this site. Today, two detached houses, *Hartings* and *Wain Wood Edge* stand where *Home Farm* farmhouse and its outbuildings once were.

Temple Farm

Temple Farm lay to the south-east of Temple Dinsley and farmed around 230 acres. These were to the north of the farmhouse, between the Hitchin Road and St Albans Highway and to the west between Wright's Lane and Hitchwood. It was demolished between 1930 and 1945. The derelict piggery designed by Lutyens *(left)* is all that remains of the farm.

Affordable 'social housing' at Preston

The tumbledown cottages at Preston were torn down in the early twentieth century and this created a problem of where local labourers and the elderly could live. A partial solution was the building of 14 estate cottages at Back Lane and Chequers Lane.

Council houses at Chequers Lane

These were augmented by council homes during the twentieth century. Most were built in the early 1920s (nos. 9 and 10 were added later) in a variety of styles and brickwork. Many of these homes are now privately owned.

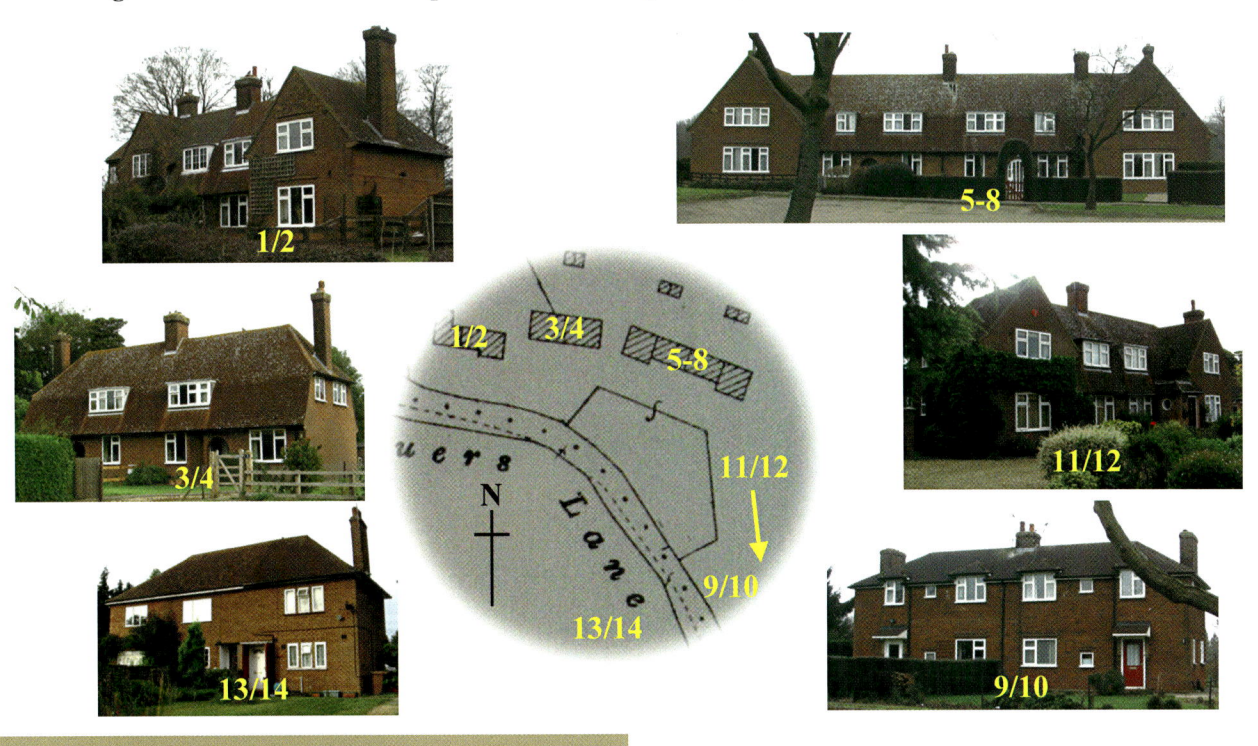

Swedish Houses, 15 - 24 Chequers Lane

After World War Two, Britain embarked on an emergency programme to quickly replace homes that had been destroyed during the war - 'Churchill's Temporary Housing Programme'. Included in this construction plan were less than 3,000 timber-built homes which were imported during 1945/46 from Sweden as 'flat-packs', to be erected on site. Ten of these were erected as council houses at Preston.

These 'factory homes' were the gift of the Swedish government for Britain's support during the war. They were supplied in sections using ultra-tough Baltic pine. In Spartan post-war Britain, they were a sensation - fireplaces in every room; fitted wardrobes in every bedroom. Many sprang up in rural settings - as an inducement to village dwellers to stay put, rather than be seduced by life in towns. They had a minimum life-span of over 150 years, but out of 2,444 built, only perhaps half remain.

They are snug and warm - being insulated by a buttercup yellow natural felt made from sheep's wool. Trust the Swedes to provide efficient means of combating the cold! Most DIY jobs can be completed using a hammer and nails.

Templars Lane

This is a small development of six single-storey homes grouped on three sides of a rectangle. By 2015, six more 'affordable' homes were built here.

Selected people of Preston and events in the village

Preston men who fought in WW1

For a small village, with a population of less than 350 in 1911, a surprising number of young men, who were born in or were living in Preston between 1914 and 1918, fought during The Great War - forty-two have been traced at the last count. This underlines how the effects of world war were felt in every British community, no matter how large or small it was. Partial lists of those who died during the conflict are to be found in St Martin's Church and on the Hitchin War Memorial. Preston School had a Roll of Honour of forty-seven former scholars who were combatants.

Arthur Chalkley was born in the late spring of 1880, the son of William and Amy. The couple were local people – William was born at Waterdell, Ippollitts and Amy in the village of Charlton. By 1881, the Chalkleys had moved from the countryside into Hitchin and for the next twenty years William worked as a brick-maker and a coal porter. Arthur Chalkley married Harriet Claridge in the summer of 1903, after a lengthy friendship – in 1901, he was recorded as a visitor to the Claridge's home at Ley Green, Kings Walden. Arthur was a drover (of sheep) and Harriet was a seventeen-year-old stone picker. The couple had one son, William Arthur (Bill), who was born at Ley Green in the winter of 1904. In 1911, the small family were living at Back Lane, Preston - and Arthur was a stockman on a farm.

When Arthur enlisted, he was living at Little Munden, a village five miles to the east of Stevenage. He was Private 4393 in the Hertfordshire Regiment, First Battalion. He was killed on 4 September 1916 (aged 36) and was buried at Knightsbridge Cemetery. Following the death of her husband, Harriet and Bill remained in Preston for the rest of their lives – living together at Crunnells Green and later at 20 Swedish Cottages, Chequers Lane. Harriet (who didn't re-marry) died in 1968 aged 84 and was buried at St Martin, Preston on 30 January.

William James Ewington was born at Chequers Lane, Preston in the spring of 1893. He was the son of William (a hay-tier) and Caroline (nee Saunders). Caroline died in the spring of 1897.

Four years later, in 1911, William and his father were lodging at *The Chequers* and working as fitter's labourers, possibly helping with the Temple Dinsley renovations. He enlisted quickly as Private 6856 in the Bedfordshire Regiment, First Battalion but died on 7 November 1914 (aged 21). He was buried at Le Touret Cemetery. William's sacrifice is noted on Hitchin's War memorial. His father, William, was living at Back Lane in 1915 and remained in Preston for the rest of his life. He died in 1936 and was buried at St Martin on 22 June.

Bill Frost in his *History of Preston CC* mentions Percy Evered (sic) - a cricketer who died during the conflict. On checking the 1911 census, **Percy Evershed** (a carpenter, born c.1883) was discovered. He and his younger brother were born at Washington, Sussex and were lodging with Thomas and Martha Peters at *The Old Forge* on Church Lane. Percy (Reg. No. G/4673) joined the 4th Battalion of the Royal Sussex Regiment and was promoted to Sergeant. He was occasionally posted back to England as a bomb-throwing instructor and during a training session (using live ammunition) his prompt and courageous action saved a Lieutenant's life. Percy's selfless act was rewarded with the Meritorious Service Medal for gallantry.

Percy was part of the British Expeditionary Force. On 28 May 1918, he died of pneumonia when he was a prisoner of war and is buried in Peronne Communal Cemetery at the Somme. He was also awarded the Victory and British medals.

Sidney Sharp was born at Breachwood Green, Kings Walden in the winter of 1885, the son of Herbert (a forester for the Stagenhoe estate) and Emily (nee Peacock of Ley Green, Kings Walden). From 1891, the Sharps were living at Back Lane, Preston until 1911 when they had moved to Chequers Lane. Sidney was also a farm labourer.

He joined the Bedfordshire Regiment, Second Battalion (Private 20818). Sidney was killed on 30 July 1916 and was buried at Thiepval Cemetery. His death is noted on the Hitchin War Memorial.

At the time, Herbert and Emily were living at 9 Council Cottages, Chequers Lane, Preston. In 1951, Herbert resided at 11 Chequers Lane. He died (aged 93) in 1957 and was buried at St Martin on 28 November.

William Jenkins was born in the summer of 1895, the son of William and Minnie (nee Boston) Jenkins – both from established Preston families. The Jenkins were living at School Lane, Preston in 1901 and 1911 and William snr., was a cowman. William, jnr, was a farm labourer.

William joined the Bedfordshire Regiment, First Battalion and was killed near the end of the War on 20 November 1918 (aged 23). He was buried at Etaples and is featured on Hitchin's War Memorial. William and Minnie lived at Hitchwood Cottages until their deaths in February 1944 and January 1962, respectively. They were buried at St Martin.

Ernest Wray *(pictured below)* was born at Preston on 8 December 1891 and was the son of Alfred and Emily (nee Currell) Wray who lived at Back Lane, from 1891. After leaving school on 26 June 1903, aged eleven, he found work as a gardener.

Almost as soon as World War One broke out, on 5 September 1914, Ern enlisted in the 3rd Battalion of the 2nd Bedfordshire Regiment No 17002. He was the first villager to die being killed in action on 24 August 1915. He was buried at Bethune Cemetery. Details of his death are etched on the Hitchin War Memorial.

John Thomas Powell was born at Preston in the spring of 1884, probably at Crunnells Green. His parents, Henry ('Harry') and Emma were born in Hertfordshire and went to Preston in the early 1880's. They were living at Back Lane in 1891 when Henry was a farm labourer. They continued to move around as in 1901 the family was at East Meon, Hampshire, where Henry was a gamekeeper. Meanwhile, John remained at Preston and in 1911 he was living with his sister, Caroline and her husband, George Peters, at Church Lane, Preston. He was a farm labourer. He enlisted with the Kings Shropshire Light Infantry (Private 26242) and was killed on 11 April 1917. He was buried at Saulty. His death is recorded on the Hitchin War Memorial.

Martin Henry Farey was the son of Amos and Mary (nee Isaacson) who married in the late autumn of 1892 when Amos was almost forty years old. Their first son, Martin arrived in the spring of 1894 at Preston. By 1901, the family had moved into Hitchin and were living at 70 Bancroft.

In August 1914, Martin joined the 7th Hertfordshire Regiment, First Battalion (Private 2211). He was sent to the Western Front in 1914 and fought at Ypres, Lens and Bethune and, after heavy shelling, he suffered wounds from which he died on 5 December 1915 (aged 21).

John William Reed was born in the summer of 1882 at Preston, the son of George and Mary (nee Thrussell). George was from Kings Walden and Mary, from Preston.

The family was living at Sootfield Green in 1891 and George was a farm worker. They had moved to Saffron Walden, Essex by 1901 where George was a gamekeeper.

John Reed enlisted in the Suffolk Regiment (Private 26766) at Melbourn, Cambridgeshire and later transferred to the Queens (Royal West Surrey) Regiment (Private G/21093). He was killed on Monday, 14 May 1917 and was buried at Flanders. He is featured on the Melbourn Roll of Honour.

Harry Edward Harper was born in Preston during the winter of 1895. He was the son of William and Sarah. By 1901 the family had relocated to Battlesden, Bedfordshire where William was working as a gamekeeper.

Harry enlisted in the Bedfordshire Sixth Battalion (Private 20056) at Ampthill, Beds. He died from wounds suffered at Flanders on 23 July 1916 (aged 21) and was buried at Heilly Station Cemetery, Somme.

His name is recorded on the Little Brickhill, Bucks. Roll of Honour.

William Barker I'Anson was the son of Albert and Eliza I'Anson and Frederick (bailiff of *Offley Holes House*) and Rose Perry. The Hitchin War Memorial includes him among the dead of WW1. The Commonwealth Graves Commission records his death at Flanders on 7 October 1916. He was a corporal (No 18850) in the Royal Fusiliers (City of London Regiment).

Ernest Ball was the grandson of William Andrews. He was born at Burgess Hill, Sussex c.1888. In 1911, he was a bricklayer living at Hitchwood Cottages. He served as a private with the 1st Battalion of the South Wales Borders (Reg No. 44364). Ernest was killed in action at Flanders, France on 10 September 1917.

(Charles) Stephen Ashton (*right*) was the son of Preston baker, Tom and Catherine.. He was born in 1884 at Stevenage and shortly afterwards the family moved to *The Old Forge* bakery at Church Lane, Preston. In order to join the army, Stephen exaggerated his age and gave himself another Christian name, Charles. After fighting in the Boer War, he volunteered in September 1914 and was appointed as Sergeant in the Hertfordshire Dragoons. In August 1915, he was sent to Palestine where he fought at Gaza and in the taking of Jerusalem. In 1917, he was transferred to Mesopotamia where he again saw action. He returned home after being de-mobbed in November 1919. Stephen married Lilian Wightman at Luton in 1920.

Henry James Armstrong (*below*) was born in September 1883, the son of Frederick and Emma (nee Kirkby) who were tenants at *Preston Hill Farm*. Henry joined the Fourth Bedfordshire Regiment in June 1916 as a Private. In 1917, he was drafted to the Western Front where he took part in the battles of the Somme, Arras, Ypres and Cambrai. He was wounded twice. He returned home and was de-mobbed in October 1919. He lived at *Elm Cottage*, Chequers Lane, with his mother, Emma, until her death in February 1929. Henry died and was buried at St Martin on 11 January 1961.

A. Carter gave his address as *The Chequers*, Preston, Hitchin when he was demobbed in February 1919. He enlisted in March 1888 and when war broke out, he was a reservist who was immediately called-up, joining the Royal Marine Light Infantry as a Second Class Warrant Officer. In August 1914, he was sent to Ostend and later served in Antwerp during the siege. In 1915, he was moved to the Dardenelles and after taking part in the Gallipoli campaign, he served in Egypt. He was then sent to Greece and finally to France, where he took part in numerous engagements.

In 1918, **Stephen Charles Andrews** was living at Jacks Hill, near Preston. He was with the Royal Engineers (Reg. No. 23250).

Arthur James Palmer was the son of Arthur and Lizzie (nee Fairey) who were living at *Hitchwood Cottages* in 1911. Arthur was born in the winter of 1892 and was a cowman. He volunteered in August 1914 and was a Private in the Hertfordshire Regiment. Because of ill health he was not sent overseas and was invalided out of the service in December 1914. By then his parents were living at Chequers Lane. Arthur married Alice Maud Thrussell at St Martin, Preston on 30 June 1917. He gave his occupation as roadman.

Walter Charles and **Henry George Peters** were born in 1894 and the spring of 1898 respectively, the sons of Henry George (a waggoner in 1911) and Caroline (nee Powell). The family was living at Church Road, Preston in 1911. **Walter** volunteered in January 1915 and was a Gunner in the Royal Field Artillery. He was sent to France in the same year and was involved in heavy fighting which included the Battles of Ypres, Loos, Arras and Cambrai. He was wounded but rejoined his Regiment and was demobbed in March 1920. **Henry** joined the 1st Buffs (East Kent) Regiment in January 1916. He was stationed at Rouen and Calais guarding the detention camps and demobilised in November 1919. On leaving the army, the brothers returned to the family home at 5 *Holly Cottages*, Back Lane, but both had left Preston by 1930. Walter married Philadelphia C Heathorn at St Martin on 22 November 1922 and the couple remained in the Hitchin area.

Sidney Charles Burton was born in 1883 and married Lavinia Louisa Cooper at Ippollitts Church in 1910. He was a chauffeur at Poynders End when he joined the Bedfordshire Regiment on 9 December 1915. From January until November 1917, he served in France with the Machine Gun Corp, 120th Company as a Private. He was discharged on 26 October 1918 as being no longer physically fit for duty, having fractured his right fibula. He received the Victory and British medals.

Frederick Woodrow was the son of Frederick and Mary Annie, and was born in Norfolk in the summer of 1891. The couple were still living in the county in 1901 when Frederick snr was a wheelwright and carpenter. Frederick jnr joined in 1916 and was assigned to Second Queen's (Royal West Surrey Regiment). That year, he was drafted to France and fought at Ypres, Passchendaele and Arras. He was invalided to England owing to ill health and when he was discharged in October 1918, he held the rank of Lance Corporal. He returned to the family home at *Holly Cottages*, Back Lane but by 1925, they had left the village.

Robert (Bob) *(below)* (born 19 April 1894), **Frank** (17 July 1899) and **Charlie Wray** (born 1884) were three of Alfred and Emily's (nee Currell) sons. **Bob** volunteered in August 1914, joining the Bedfordshire Regiment as a Private and was sent to France in 1915. He fought in the battles of Festubert, Arras, Albert and Vimy Ridge and throughout the Retreat and Advance of 1918. During his career, he attained the rank of Lance Corporal and was wounded three times. He was demobbed in December 1919 and received the Military Medal. Bob married Elizabeth (Lizzie) May Jenkins at St Mary, Hitchin on 18 November 1922. The couple moved to Peters Green, Kimpton where they had twelve children.

Frank Wray *(below)* joined the Bedfordshire Regiment in 1917 as a Private and was sent to the Western Front in that year. He fought in the Battles of Ypres, Cambrai, the Somme, Neuve Chapelle and the Retreat and advance of 1918 when he was wounded. After the Armistice he was sent into Germany with the Army of Occupation serving on the Rhine. He returned to England in 1920 and was demobbed in April. Frank married Margaret Campbell at St Martin on 2 June 1926. The couple lived at 9 Council Cottages, Chequers Lane, Preston and had four children. Frank (37) died from influenza and was buried at St Martin on 15 October 1936.

Charlie Wray *(below)* enlisted about three weeks after the outbreak of war on 16 August 1914. He was a Private in the Bedfordshire First Regiment (No. 7708). In September 1915, he was back in England having been gassed. He transferred to the Bedfordshire Territorial Force (No. 201481) where he served as an Acting Corporal. He was demobbed on 20 February 1920 after receiving three medals.

Arthur Robert Boreham. Arthur was from Ley Green but had moved to Back Lane, Preston by 1918. His son, Reginald Arthur, was at Preston School on 7 January 1919. Arthur's Reg. No. was 2686 and he served as an Able Seaman in the Royal Navy.

Charles Alfred Biles was a game keeper who lived at Keepers Lodge on the Kings Walden Road, Preston. He joined the Royal Garrison Artillery on 1 August 1916 (31) and then the Royal Scots Artillery Regiments (Reg No 111343) and held the rank of Gunner. Charles served at Salonika. He contracted malaria on 17 July 1916 and was awarded an Army pension until 23 November 1920. He received the Victory and British medals.

In 1911, **William Claxton** was a gamekeeper at Cockenhoe, Herts., aged 27. He was married with two children. Five years later, in 1916, William Claxton was the licensee of *The Chequers* inn at Preston. By 1918 he was serving as a Private in the Queens Regiment Labour Corps and the Royal Fusiliers (Reg No 406011). He received the Victory and the British medals. After being demobbed, he and his family lived at Wain Wood until at least 1930.

Edward Peters *(right)* was born at Preston in 1885. He was the son of Thomas and Martha.

Clearly from his uniform, he was involved the Great War - perhaps in a medical capacity.

William Swain *(right)* was born at Preston in 1889. He was the son of George and Mary Swain. He served with the 4th Bedfordshire Rifles and was awarded the Military Medal.

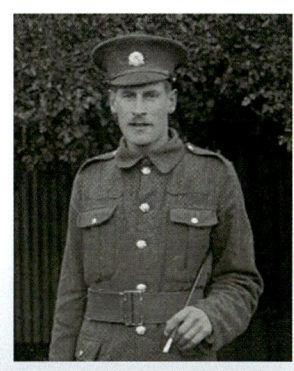

Arthur Robert Crawley was the grandson of Henry Crawley and was born at Preston in around 1898. In 1918, he was living at Back Lane and was a Private with the Suffolks and then the 2nd London Regiment' the Royal Fusiliers (Reg. No. 12435). Arthur joined in 1917 and was drafted to the Western Front. He saw heavy fighting at Ypres, Cambrai and the Somme where he was wounded. He then served in the Palestine Offensive at Jaffa. Arthur was demobbed in April 1920 and received the General Service and Victory medals.

William Frederick Cullum. In 1911, William (born around 1882 in Leicestershire) was a married chauffeur living at *Temple Dinsley Lodge*. He joined the RAF (Reg No 225157). In 1918, William was living at *Kiln Wood Cottage*, Preston.

George William Garner was living at Poynders End in 1918. He served as a driver with 7th Sec No 3 Army Aux (Horse Company) ASC (Reg. No. TI 2679) and received the Victory medal.

John Garner was born in 1889, the horse-keeper son of farm bailiff George Garner who was living at *Poynders End Farm* in 1911. John married Daisy Darton at Ippollitts Church on 20 January 1912. Three years later, a son, William Arthur Garner, was born on 15 March 1915, when John and Daisy were living at *Hitchwood Cottages*. John enlisted at Bedford on 5 December 1915 as a Private in the Northamptonshire Regiment (Reg. No. 25565).

There is a lengthy record of John's service online which includes his time with the 1st Yorks. and Lancs. Regiment (31852); promotion to Lance Corporal and three months leave from June until September 1916 to recover from injuries to his left ankle and right leg (which resulted in 30% disablement). He was demobbed on 3 July 1919 with a pension and the Victory and British medals. John and Daisy were at *Poynders End Farm* in 1919. John died at Offley on 17 April 1962 and was buried at St Martin, Preston.

John Murphy was living at Hill End in 1918. He was a Private in the 432nd Agriculture Company Corps at Kempston Barracks, Beds. He was in France from 26 October 1915 and received the Victory, British and Star medals.

Ernest Payne *(below)* was a general labourer living with his parents, Thomas and Mary Payne, at Poynders End in 1911. He joined the RAF and was shown as living at Crunnells Green in 1918.

Christopher Thomas Peters was born at Preston in around 1881 to Thomas and Martha Peters. He was a Private in DVC (Reg No 12066) and his home was at Chequers Lane in 1918.

Algernon William Sims was the son of the head gardener at Temple Dinsley and was living at Preston in 1911. He was a Sergeant Mechanic in the RAF and in 1918, gave his address as *The Cottage*, Preston.

Frederick Shaw was thirty-six-years-old, and a butler living at 2 Markham Square, Kings Road, Chelsea when he enlisted on 13 December 1916. Three years earlier, he married Grace Naylor at Chelsea Register Office, but by 1918, the couple had no children. Frederick served as a Gunner in the Royal Horse and Royal Field Artillery (Reg. No. 198076). He was demobbed in 1919 and lived at Preston until at least 1930. As he lived in Ippollitts Parish, possibly he was a butler at Temple Dinsley.

Sidney Smith was living at Poynders End in 1918. He was a Lance Corporal with the Military Mounted Police 14th Corp, Headquarters (Reg. No. P2900).

Leonard Charles Smith was living at Poynders End in 1918. He was a Private in the 4th Bedfordshire Transport Section serving in France from 2 October 1915. He received the Victory, Star and British medals.

John Swain was a private in the Bedfordshire, Northumberland and Suffolk regiments (Nos. 27031; 41684 and 42354 respectively). He received the Victory and British medals. A John Swain is noted as living at *Holly Cottages*, Back Lane Preston from 1920 to 1930 and Frederick Woodrow was also living in the cottages in 1920. Perhaps these two soldiers were rewarded for their service with accommodation in these estate cottages.

Percy Sharp *(right)* was living at Poynders End when he joined the 23rd (Duke of Cambridge's) Middlesex Regiment as a Private (Reg. No. 20249). He received the Victory and the British medals. In 1929, he and his wife Lucy were living at *Hitchwood Cottages*, but by 1951 they were living in the council houses on the north side of Chequers Lane.

Oliver Henry D. Vickers of Temple Dinsley (son of Douglas) served as a Second Lieutenant in the RAF.

Frederick Walker was a horse-keeper at Little Hill End, near Preston in 1911, living with his father-in-law, wife (Alice) and daughter (Violet). He joined the Bedfordshire Labour Corp as a Private (Reg Nos 19300 and 240207) and in 1918 he was with the 432nd Agriculture Company, Labour Corps, Kempston Barracks, Beds. He received the Victory and British medals. Frederick and Alice lived at 6 Chequers Lane in the 1950s. He died in September 1969, aged 85.

John Henry Walkden was born in around 1891 and served as a Private in the Rifle Brigade (Reg No 15415) and the 80th Machine Gun Corp (95814). When he enlisted on 9 December 1915, he was a grocer's assistant living at 50 Mornington Road, Leytonstone East, London. He received the Victory and British medals and was discharged on 24 March 1919 as being unfit for duty having contracted malaria. John's next-of-kin was his mother Mary who was living at Preston and the address to which his war badge and certificate were sent was *St Martin's Place*, Preston.

Frederick Woodrow (born 11 June 1884) was a game keeper of *Hollybush Cottage*, Kings Walden when he enlisted, aged 39, on 31 May 1916. A little more than six weeks later, he married Mary Ann Cridge at Hitchin Register Office on 18 July 1916. They had five children born between 1902 and 1910. Frederick was in the Queens Regiment Labour Corp (Reg. Nos. 47405 and 73987) and served at Ypres, Passchendaele and Arras. He was invalided to England because of ill health in 1918 and discharged as unfit for duty in the October when he was living at *Holly Cottages*, Preston. He was still residing there in 1920.

Preston and World War Two

> The tranquil life of Preston was not untouched by the Second World War. German bombers and fighter escorts droned overhead en route to Luton, Birmingham and Coventry. The village saw many new faces - evacuated children, Land Army girls, soldiers billeted nearby and prisoners of war working in the fields. In the distance, to the south, a glow in the night's sky proclaimed the latest blitz of the nation's capital - 'You could see the searchlights in the sky over London'.
>
> Two of Preston's sons died in the conflict.

The menace from the sky

During the six years of war, the Hitchin rural area (including Preston) received eleven VI Flying Bombs, four V2 rockets, 6,527 incendiary bombs, 27 oil bombs, 8 parachute mines, three phosphorous bombs and two fire pot bombs - 'a formidable total for a rural area'. 792 homes were damaged, but only nine were beyond repair.

The precautions adopted in towns also applied to Preston - Rebecca Cook (nee Brown), of *Pond Farm*, Preston: *We were told we must now blackout every window...my sisters had made black curtains and dark curtains and we had a big board we put up over the kitchen window...we were very careful about that....(there was) an Air Raid Warden coming around and checking up just to see that there were no chinks of light showing anywhere.*

'In the old farm house we didn't even have any electricity so we used to take candles to bed. We'd read by candle light making sure that the curtains were well drawn.'

Ann Fenton (nee Middleditch): *'Oh yes the black out - all windows were covered in black material, and tape criss-crossed over the windows. Lights were not allowed to be shown - cars and bikes had to have their lights showing and a contraption was fixed so that lights only shone directly in front of where you were going. Candles were at a premium everywhere. Fuel for lamps was a scarce commodity for those who didn't have wood stoves to cook on or electricity - the latter was not in every house in the village.'*

Rebecca: *'There was one air raid warning siren at Hitchin, another at Luton and another somewhere else and we got to know them by their names because they all made different noises. I remember calling one 'Wailing Willie' and one 'Screaming Lizzie'. We'd hear the Hitchin one go up and then the Luton one. It was just part of our life, the air raid warnings, and then you sort of wondered if the bombers would come over - and quite often they did. Sometimes as we were cycling home (from Hitchin) the air raid sirens would go and we would pedal like fury to make sure we got home.'*

There were batteries with searchlights lighting up the night sky at Whitwell and Chapel Foot (on the Hitchin to St Pauls Walden Road).

Rebecca: *'My brothers did start to enthusiastically dig us an air raid shelter but it never got finished. No, we didn't do anything to shelter during an air raid...'*

At Princess Helena College, (PHC) Temple Dinsley, although Preston had been designated 'safe', the school took precautions. Its Tudor cellars were cleared of junk, swept clean and whitewashed, making bomb-proof shelters where girls could sleep and gas masks hung. Two hundred and ninety-seven windows and nine skylights had to be blacked out.

The headmistress, Miss Prain, herself, sewed all the curtains. After France fell, the gardeners roofed over a chalk pit in a wood nearby, to be known as 'Hitler's Hall', where the girls and staff and plenty of tinned food could be housed, and they installed electric light.

At PHC it was reported that three bombs landed on fields not far away (one burst, the rest were duds) and an abandoned German plane or two, and three V1 rockets.

Rebecca: *I remember sitting at night when it was dark and the airplanes going over - we could hear ours going. You could almost count them as they were going to war. Then sometimes you would hear a plane with quite a different sound and Dad would say, "That's a German" and we would wait and pray "let it go over" and (it) kept going. Then sometimes we would hear a bomb come whistling down and it sounded just as if it was coming on the house. The next morning, my brother said, "Come on, lets go look where the bomb landed" and we went across and there was this enormous hole in one of our fields and we found that quite exciting. One fell on the local blacksmith but not on his house. I can't remember anyone being killed - we had two or three on our farm, but none on the house.*

Ann: *'I remember watching the German planes coming over in broad day-light and bombing Luton Airport and Vauxhall Motors and the dog fight and anti aircraft guns shooting down the enemy. The Doodle Bugs - one fell in a field not far from Keepers Lodge and on the way to Kings Walden - made quite a crater! The VE bombs were scary as well, doing lots of damage everywhere they landed. Dad was in the Home Guard, like most of the men who were too old to go into combat'.*

Rebecca: *My father was in the Home Guard. They were all given their tin hats and their uniform and had drill. I suppose it was on the playing field. Then they would have turns in fire watching. All the older men in the village who weren't called up would go and watch for incendiary bombs being dropped all over the place and they had sand bags with which to put them out. They used to have a sort of crossed barriers. They put them across the road so if anyone was coming along they would say, "Who goes there" and stop them in the dead of night and see who they were. Every single sign-post was removed. I remember one hot summer afternoon (at Hitchin)...suddenly we heard planes up above. We looked up and there was a German plane and English fighter planes sort of dodging round it, I think they were Hurricanes, and we looked up in horror because they were just above us and we could see them. And they did shoot the poor chap down and then of course, my brothers, being big brothers, went across to find the airplane and all the pieces of it. There was a lot of bombing over Luton - the Vauxhall works and so on. We used to hear them, the crashes. And we could see late at night looking down towards London and actually see the sky red at night from the Blitz.'*

A Wellington bomber crashed and burnt out at Sootfield Green. The RAF cleaned up the site but local lads searched the spot for 'odd bits like bullets'. On 30 August 1940, the Germans flew a sortie of around twenty Heinkel bombers escorted by thirty Messerschmitts against Luton airport and the Vauxhall works. Just short of Luton, they were intercepted by fighters from Northolt and North Weald. During the ensuing dogfight, a Messerschmitt crashed at Whiteway Bottom, Kimpton. Its pilot was killed and was buried at Hitchin. According to eyewitnesses, a British fighter crashed in a garden at Harpenden.

> "We looked up and there was a German plane and English fighter planes sort of dodging round it..."

At 20.00 on the night of 8 April 1941, a Defiant fighter out of Biggin Hill, opened fire on another Heinkel (part of a raid on Coventry) above Whitwell (near Preston). The bomber was shot down and crashed at Bendish House but not before the surviving crew bailed out and parachuted down in or near Kings Walden Park. They were quickly rounded up and taken prisoner. The body of the plane's observer was found the next morning at Duxleys Wood, Breachwood Green still attached to its parachute. He, too, was interred at Hitchin.

Then, on the following night, a Junkers 88 crashed at *Preston Hill Farm*. It was making a bombing run on Fort Dunlop at Birmingham when it was fired on by a night fighter. It was 'like someone throwing a handful of stones against a tin wall'. The pilot turned towards the nearest point on the continental coast - which took his plane over Hertfordshire. Unable to keep airborne, the pilot ordered his crew to bail out.

The 'line of washing' came down in a line from Hartling to Kings Walden Park. One of the crew was picked up by a bus running between Hitchin and Luton. A RAF officer on the bus took charge of him and ordered the bus driver to Luton Police Station. Three others of the crew landed at Hartlington, Butterfield Green and Frogmore. Mrs Fisher, who lived at Bendish Lodge on Lilley Bottom Road, spoke of her fright as a German walked past her home shouting at the top of his voice. The last man to bail out was found by Hitchin Fire Brigade who were trying to put out the fire of the burning Junkers.

Some wreckage of the Junkers was recovered from *Preston Hill Farm*, including the engines, but it was believed more was to be found.

Several years later, Peter Stanley of RAF Henlow (seven miles to the north of Preston) rang David Steadman to ask where he might hire a JCB locally for a dig at the crash site. When the new excavation began, it was discovered that the subsoil was chalky, but grey where the plane had burnt out. Most of the wreckage found was jangled pieces of aluminium sheet, some pierced by bullets. The dig lasted three hours, guided by Stanley's metal detector. They found live bullets, hydraulic gear for operating the flaps and the armature from a motor or a generator.

Robert Sunderland: *'A doodlebug fell in the corner of Hearnsfield Wood, Preston Hill Farm. Parts of it were still there when I worked for Fred Maybrick. There was another one that came down between Austage End and Preston.'*

Of soldiers based around Preston

PHC remained unscathed by the turmoil of war until April 1942 when some Canadian soldiers took down and made away with a lead gazelle - one of two mounted on the main gate pillars.

At Hitchwood, about a mile south-east of Preston, two camps ('North' and 'South') were established to train soldiers for fighting overseas and the D-Day landings. A local builder from Hitchin built huts there, which housed some of the men. The remains of their brick ovens can still be seen *(below)*.

Frank Thomas recorded his experiences at a Hitchwood Camp: *'About the middle of August 1942, a number of us younger soldiers were posted to 39th L.A.A. Regiment which was in camp at Hitchwood, a wood about 3 miles from Hitchin, Herts. The regiment was preparing to go overseas, but where no one knew. When I joined the 39th Light A/A (Anti-Aircraft) Regiment..... I was allocated to 111th Battery D Troop. I arrived at Hitchwood in time for six weeks of infantry training before more serious A/A training for overseas. The infantry training stood us in good stead when in August 1944 we were ordered to leave our Bofors guns behind and go into the front line as an infantry regiment.*

At the time I joined, intensive training was going on, not just with anti-aircraft guns, but also infantry training in case we had to resort to this.

There was a large common opposite our camp where this training was carried out. Not only was there the usual assault course, and training in tactics, but also at times we would form a line in a clear part of the common, and be ordered to proceed straight ahead. Whatever obstacle lay on our path we must not deviate from a straight line. Our motto was "Get through it". I have been thankful for that tough course many times in my life when things had been difficult. What did St Paul say? "I have fought the good fight, I have kept the faith" Yes he went straight ahead. Alas, I have often failed, and yet often in difficult times I am thankful for Hitchwood.'

In 1943, Temple Dinsley was almost requisitioned until it was saved by an outbreak of measles. However, the Lodge and some land next to the games field were occupied by army vehicles and mobile guns. Then, girls and soldiers ogled each other during lacrosse, tennis and gun practice.

Rebecca: *'Army lorries used to come down our little road and then it divided at the bottom and we'd go out to wave to the soldiers....We had the Military Police - they were actually stationed only about two miles away, yes we did see quite a lot of them about.'*

The 'Evacuated' come to Preston

Ann: *'Preston was also one of the places to which evacuees came, to get away from the destruction of London. The children were scared, lonely and some had lost everything from the bombing and were outfitted with clothing, shoes, etc., for the changes of weather. They were treated well in the village and some stayed after the war and made the area their home together with their parents who survived the bombing and destruction of their homes.'*

The Preston School logbook provides occasional comments about the life of children before and during the war: 3 February 1939 - *'W. Peters fitted gas masks'.*

Rebecca: *'I remember we were all issued with gas masks. We had to go into the Village Hall to be fitted - to be shown how to put them on. And I remember I had a baby sister and that you had to put the baby right inside a thing, a great big thing on the table and mother looking at that and saying, 'Never will I put my baby in there!' She was just horrified.*

And then I remember one of my big sisters making cases. We used up any old things that we could cut up, old curtains or fabric, or whatever. She made us very smart cases with a strap because we had to take them to school every day and that just became part of our uniform, with our satchels and we always got an order mark if we forgot them. We used to put them on top of the cupboard when we got to school and then every Friday morning have Gas Mask Drill.

We had to go through and all put our gas masks on and pull funny faces at each another and the teacher would come round testing to see that - putting their fingers in the sides. Whether they would have been any use, I really don't know.'

Ann: *'All the children were issued gas masks and ID's. I still remember my ID number which we dutifully took with us whenever we were outside the home and especially to school where we had regular air raid drills and were taught the use of the gas mask and where to go in case of an air raid to the shelters or the safest place.'*

Preston School logbook: 4 September 1939: *'School should have re-opened today, but war having begun, I have closed the School 'til further orders.'* 12 September 1938: *'School re-opens today. We shall work in double shifts. This week the village children will attend from 09.00 'til 13.00 and the evacuated children from 13.15 to 17.15.'* This arrangement lasted a fortnight - *'The School will from today be open for the usual hours, the evacuated children being provided with accommodation from PHC'*.

In March 1940, the senior children went to schools in Hitchin and Preston School became a centre for the education of Infant and Juniors Mixed. Its students included several from nearby towns and villages such as Langley and Stevenage. In all, during the six years of war, Preston School admitted 171 new children. During the following six years, there were ninety-nine new admissions - which illustrates the remarkable turnover of scholars during the war. Log Book, 2 September 1940: *'There are now 23 village children and eleven evacuees'*. First Mrs Bailey was in charge of the temporary residents, then Mrs Devlin, then Miss Saunders. Intriguingly, on 26 February 1841, there is a note that, *'The children will be taken to Church for Ash Wednesday - the Jewish evacuees who do not wish to go, will be left in charge of a teacher'*. By 15 September 1941, the School was caring for forty-seven children, twenty-five from Herts. and twenty-two evacuees.

Sadly for some children during this time, a deadly threat was not only from across the English Channel. Two girls, Evelyn Jane Fuller of 2 Council Cottages, Langley and Pamela Hammond (daughter of Ernest Hammond of Back Lane, Preston) died of diphtheria.

Rebecca: *'There was a boys school from London. I remember Mr. Hinds the Headmaster coming with all these boys, they were staying in a big old College in the village and they took over our school for a time.*

Nothing was really happening to worry them in London it didn't start until at least the next year from I remember. So they went home. I remember then we had a lot of evacuees came to live in the College and they were very harum-scarum and they used to put this gas mask in it's box but put an apple or their lunch or conkers, anything, they were all in the gas masks. What it did to them I can't imagine! They used to fling them about. Yes, there were quite a number of evacuees. We, being such a big family, (there were eleven of us) just hadn't got any room to take any more but

"...any families that had got a spare room, the children were just left there, poor little things."

any families that had got a spare room, the children were just left there, poor little things. And mother used to feel so sorry for them and we used to invite them and take them along to Sunday School and mother used to say, 'Bring them home to tea.' So invariably we would have extras to tea from the village and to us they were just other children and sometimes we laughed at them and their funny ways. They were Londoners and they seemed to almost speak a different language to us and we were country children. But we were kind to them. Yes, I remember taking them for walks, primrosing and so on around the fields.'*

'Land Girls', POWs and youth workers

Despite the war, crops still had to sown and harvested and many of the local labourers were in the trenches or otherwise engaged in the war effort. So, a motley work force was pressed into service. Many single young women, including my mother, were swept from the towns and cities of England to do the labouring work of men. In all, there were ninety thousand Land Girls. Mum was No. 37,296. She worked at Ladygrove Farm *(she is standing far left, below with other land girls)*. One minute she was at St Barts., London, the next, 'I found myself in winter-time wearing wellingtons, grading potatoes in the snow, with a tarpaulin over us in the middle of a field in Hertfordshire - our hands were awfully cold'.

When the world was turned on its head, the land girls learnt the equality which was thrust upon them. Farmers tested them by assigning them routine, menial and back-breaking jobs such as muck-spreading, sowing potatoes, cutting thistles before the harvest and topping and tailing turnips. Working in the chill of winter and the summer's heat, they battled against mud or dust all year round.

Ann: *'There were land girls from London and other bombing targets who came and worked on the farms, both in the fields and dairies. Some of them had never been to the country before, so they were teased quite a bit but they were essential, as the men, who were old enough, were called up to serve in the various forces to fight the enemy and help protect England.'*

Margaret: *'My sister (Doris Harper) joined the Land Army and worked at Castle Farm'.*

Donald Sunderland: *'My mother (who was born in Fulham, London) came to Preston to work as a Land Girl at Castle Farm in 1940. I believe she lodged with Mrs Worthington. She met my father (who lived at 'The Wilderness') and they married at St Martin'.*

Rebecca: *'And then of course we had the Prisoners of War, the Italians and the Germans to help us on the farm. The Italians were always so cheery and singing and quite happy and tried to talk to us if we went down the field. You know now-a-days they would look on that as highly dangerous. I remember once, my sister and I we just were a bit late and we said, 'Oh, let's take a day off' and we actually played truant. We went down to the field and there was this gang of Italians, they were cutting hedges down and having a bonfire and burning it and they talked to us. Then they realised what we were doing and they raised their eyebrows and said, "Oh, you stay from school?". And we went and got some potatoes and roasted them in their bonfire!'*

'They were brought to us in lorries each day. Some of them were a bit resentful I'm afraid. I remember having a German one and well of course they would be resentful but some of them perhaps thought they were a cut above doing menial farm work. I remember we set them hedge cutting, at least my father did, and they cut it nearly down to the ground in a sort of fury I suppose at being set to work. But we treated them well. My mother always used to send them out some extra pudding or cake or something when they were having their lunch and we'd give them apples - we had fruit around the farm. Compared with how our poor men ... I remember seeing a picture in the daily paper of poor skeletons of our prisoners and Belsen and so on. Then a picture of the German prisoners and the Italians alongside looking so fat and well and well fed, and happy, I suppose, because they were out of the danger.'

Margaret: *'My father, Frank Harper, used to have Italian and German POW's working in Wain Wood cutting trees down for logs.'*

The Headmaster of PHC recalled that each year, a party of boys from Watford Grammar School *(shown below)* were employed to harvest crops on nearby farms. *'They wore holes in their trousers and socks which the Headmistress, Miss Prain, patched.'*

One of these boys was Richard Hughes: *'I was a pupil at Watford Boys Grammar School until 1943 and to help the war effort, the School arranged to assist in the harvesting at local farms near Preston for four weeks during the summer holidays starting in 1940/41.*

'As our base, we stayed at Princess Helena College for either two weeks or four weeks depending on one's choice - the first two weeks were for cutting and the second two weeks for threshing. Each boy was allocated a farm with other boys. During our spare time, we played cricket against the local village team, and joined in local village dances.'

'I remember seeing my first Flying Fortresses as they flew over the farm where I was working. I cannot remember whether it was 1942 or 1943 but I will never forget the sight of these fantastic aircraft (there were three to be exact).'

The girls of PHC helped out on the farms, uprooting charlock, thistles and other weeds which competed with turnips or clover. Each summer term for a week, a lorry took them to the fields to pick potatoes. All the way there and back they yelled a song about pink pyjamas.

Rebecca: 'School girls were given a week off in the autumn to help with potato picking. Instead of half term, everybody went potato picking and lorries used to come and pick them up. I mean we helped our own father but lorries used to come into town and take you out to which ever farms wanted you. I don't know how much use we were but I hope we were good. Because there were no farm workers you see. We used to get pocket money, I think, for doing it.

We ploughed up all our dear old meadows (at Pond Farm) that we loved and suddenly everything went under the plough. And then tractors came into being because up until then we'd had horses and then tractors came. And, yes every inch was ploughed up and you know we were really self sufficient then. Often ships bringing in food would get bombed and anyway they were all used for the war, transporting troops and so on, all the ships ... so we never saw an orange or a banana or any of the citrus fruits that were imported or grapes, unless they were home grown. We farmed mainly sheep and cattle.

My brother left school the minute he could and he took over the farm. I had a younger brother but he wasn't well - he could help, but he couldn't drive a tractor because he was too little. We girls learnt as soon as we could manage to drive - my brother taught us how to. I remember starting a tractor. Yes, we used to help all through the harvest, especially in the holidays and when I went back to school I used to be envious to hear of what my friends had been up to because we were just helping all the time - working all through the end of July and August and into September. But it was just a way of life. I think we only had one tractor at first. But it was only used when you were carting corn. You see in those days we didn't have the combine harvester - that didn't come until towards the end of the war. So we cut the corn with a binder, then they were sheaves and we had to go round and set them up in what we called shooks, or in some parts they called them stooks. Then you came round with a tractor and trailer - well we used to do it with a horse and cart then when we had a tractor, with a tractor and a trailer and stop at every stook. So we girls were roped in for that as soon as you were strong enough. It had a very hard clutch that you had to hold down to stop and as soon as you had strength to sit on the seat and reach to hold this clutch down, we were roped in to drive the tractor. We quite enjoyed it in the end. And then sometimes it was quite a long way back to the rick yard and then perhaps one of the men would come and take over then or let us drive and they would sit with us and see that we got safely through the gates and things. But as soon as we were big enough we worked. We 'little old girls' of fourteen weren't very big or strong, but we were always roped in for anything that was possible, whether moving the cattle from one field to another or from one farm to another. We all used to go out and help.'

Of food and rationing

Ann: 'Coupons were issued for each household for essential food like butter, sugar etc. and clothing coupons for essentials. Rationing hit every one. Some food stuffs were hard to come by and garden allotments sprang up all over the place, so that we could grow vegetables. There were quite a few up Back Lane where the School is now. Each family were allotted so many feet - the harvest was shared by all.'

Rebecca: 'Our rations were sufficient and we used to eat lots of vegetables. Sweets were rationed. First of all they were just non-existent and then they arrived, so we had one choc bar a week, - you imagine! One little two ounce bar a week. I think most people could afford their bar of chocolate. We used to eat raw carrots and lots of apples and pears because being on the farm we were more fortunate than most because we did had all that free fruit. I think most people in the country had some sort of fruit tree.

I have to admit farmers came off better than most people because we also had our own eggs and rabbits to help out the rations. My brothers went shooting. They would shoot rabbits and pheasants if they happened to come across one. So the rations were helped out. It was easier to make a bigger joint go round a lot of people rather than trying to eke out because we had two ounces I think of butter each, a week! Yes, we had these coupons - coupons for clothes.'

Robert: My grandparent's smallholding was about two acres. I well remember Grandpa being very concerned later on that the land would be taken out of his hands and farmed by someone else. They kept goats, ducks and chickens and one of Taylor's farm labourers, Mr Nunn, who lived at Pond Farm after the war, cultivated quite a large area for vegetables. The produce was shared. Mr Bonfield (a Whitwell milkman) would come along with his little Ferguson T20 and side-cutter to take a crop of hay off much of the rest. Grandpa also tried sugar-beet but the rats ate the lot. We got milk from the goats (and manure). Billy kids went to a Letchworth Bacon Factory. Eggs were stored in an isinglass solution. Lots of jam was made from our plums and fruit picked along the hedges. Apples, pears were stored until about March. Grandma pickled much of the garden produce and baked her own bread. They were nearly self-sufficient and did not suffer the worst of the privations of the war.

The Preston Hill "murder" and robbery (1864)

(Left) The bottom of Preston Hill c. 1913 and *(right)* the corner today

The Preston Hill "murder" was widely reported - even *The Times* carried the story. To set the scene: it was a cold, frosty, dark night in January 1864. The right-angled corner where the incident took place is at the bottom of a steep hill. Here, the road was only twelve feet wide.

Edward Foreman was a 35-year-old miller from the nearby village of Charlton. At about 15.00 on Monday afternoon, 11 January 1864, he set out from home in his mule and cart to collect outstanding monies owed by his customers who lived in a circuit between Offley and Kings Walden. Foreman was carrying £2 and some silver change in a purse. He collected £6 from three customers. Just before 18.00, he called at a Frogmore inn where he had gin and water – 'I don't think he was quite sober'. At *The Red Lion*, Preston Ebenezer Foster served Foreman with two pints of beer.

Just after 19.00, at the corner of Preston Green, Frederick Sharp saw Foreman in his cart : 'He was trotting the mule...and the mule was galloping when he had got about fifty yards'. It was reportedly well known that 'when (Foreman) was a little elevated, he drove very fast - the mule being as fleet as a deer'.

At Gosmore, an employee of Foreman, James Wildman, saw the mule and cart with no occupant– 'The mule was galloping...not seeing (Foreman) in the cart, I thought something was wrong...I examined the reins and found that the near rein was wrapped twice around the loop on the pad so that it would not work'.

Thomas Currell found Foreman's prone figure at the bottom of Preston Hill at around 19.30 as he was walking from his home at Gosmore to Preston. Foreman's feet were on the rails and his head on the road. 'I stopped and halloed to him and said "Wake up. Don't lie here". I thought he was drunk and asleep'. After a few minutes, Currell continued his walk up Preston Hill. Near *The Chequers* he met the hay binder, Samuel Wabey (33), and his son-in-law, Joseph Harmer (14) both of whom lived at Gosmore. The pair had been working for Mr Brown at Preston and then went to the *Red Lion*. Currell told them, 'There is a man lying at the bottom of Preston Hill and I can't wake him'.

A little after 21.00, Currell returning home saw Foreman still lying in the road – but he had been moved – he was now lying on his back. He met a man leading a horse and told him, 'There is a man drunk as a pig at the bottom of the hill'.

An hour later, at 22.00, Frederick Mead was walking from Stevenage and also came across Foreman: 'I felt his face and hands and they were nearly cold. He was still breathing...I put my hand to the back part of his head to raise it up and my hand was covered in blood'. Mead rushed to Wain Wood and roused his father-in-law who got out his horse and cart while Mead went on to *The Chequers* to enlist more helpers. Using lanterns, John French and Joshua Farmer lifted the body into the cart and it was taken to Hitchin Infirmary. Although Foreman was still alive, his skull was fractured and he died at 03.30 on Tuesday morning. The attending doctor was unsure as to the cause of death: 'It was impossible to decide whether it was from a fall from a cart on a hard road or a blow. It appeared to be done by a blunt instrument'. Foreman's purse and money were missing.

The *Hertfordshire Mercury* led with the story that Foreman had been 'attacked and robbed by some men, being so violently abused that he died from his injuries'.

A few days later, after a reporter had visited the scene, the *Mercury* modified its opinion, pointing out the steepness of Preston Hill; the sharpness of the bend; that the near rein would not have worked and that thus the galloping mule could have drawn the cart up the bank (where there was a mark), throwing Foreman out. As accidental death was now suspected, attention was switched to the possibility of a robbery being committed. Since Samuel Wabey was 'absent from home', he was the main suspect.

Wabey's movements after his conversation with Currell were traced. He drank two pints at *The White Horse,* Hitchin at 20.00 and asked for change of a sovereign. When he arrived, 'he appeared agitated'. At about 21.00 he paid his landlord's wife six shillings in owed rent. On Wednesday morning, Wabey and Harmer caught a train from Hitchin to Hatfield. From there they walked to St Albans where Wabey stayed at a lodging house, spoke of the Preston contretemps and 'appeared in a good deal of trouble' to a room-mate. He and Harmer then returned to Hatfield.

Meanwhile, on Tuesday, Wabey's wife had bought an umbrella for 2/4d at a Hitchin drapers shop, paying for it with a sovereign. Questioned about this at her home by the police on the following Sunday, she refused to say from where she had obtained the money. A search revealed four more sovereigns and a receipt for ten shillings. The previous day, a blood-stained 'slop' (jacket) belonging to Wabey had also been found at the house. Earlier, on Friday, Wabey and Harmer went to Hitchin Police Station where they were both taken into custody. Harmer denied any involvement in the robbery but eventually said that he had seen Wabey 'pull a purse out of the man's pocket...(saying) "I've got the ------- money"'. 'A great crowd followed Wabey as he was removed to the lock-up and all sorts of rumours were afloat in the town as to the real confession of the boy (Harmer).'

At his trial, Wabey was found guilty and was given a jail sentence of four years. Harmer was discharged.

There are points of interest to be gleaned from this episode. The Temple Dinsley clock is mentioned in the news stories. Without this information how else would we know the way in which the clock regulated villagers' lives? The clock could be seen from Preston Green and was heard at the bottom of Preston Hill. The clock face and chimes were therefore an essential part of the sights and sounds of Preston. The clock was destroyed by fire in 1888.

When studying family history, we may wonder how personality characteristics may be passed on. Thomas Currell was my great grandfather. When asked why he did nothing to help Foremen, he replied, 'I helped a drunken man a few weeks ago and when I got him up he abused me and I said I would never help another drunken man'. When my wife read this report she said, 'That's your Dad speaking!'. Harbouring a grudge is evidently a family trait - but I am *so* relieved that it wasn't Thomas who robbed the body!

Mary Woodhams (nee Chalkley) and Preston School

Mary was born on 20 February 1913, the daughter of Arthur and Harriet Chalkley. Earlier, in 1911, the family was living in one of the tumble-down, two-up/two-down cottages at Back Lane, Preston and Arthur was working as a stockman. A son, William Arthur (Bill) Chalkley, had been born on 4 October 1904.

Tragedy was to strike this small family. During the Great War, Arthur had enlisted with the Hertfordshire Regiment and he was killed (aged 36) on 4 September 1916 and buried at Knightsbridge Cemetery. When Mary started at Preston School on 13 March 1918, her father's name was crossed through and Harriet's name was inserted.

There is an enchanting and unmistakable photographic record of Mary at Preston School:

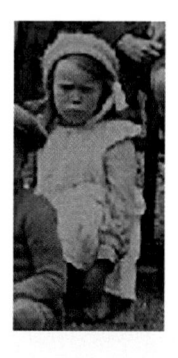

On Saturday 17 July 1925, a Country Dance competition was held in the Priory grounds at Hitchin in which seven teams competed.

The team from Preston School gained a first-class certificate and the silver cup awarded to the best team gaining 94 marks out of 100. Mary *(right)* was a member of this team.

One year later, Mary's mother, Harriet, started work as a cleaner at Preston School on 16 July 1926, earning seven shillings a week. Mary left the school on 13 April 1927.

In the summer of 1937, she married William Arthur Woodhams in the Hitchin area (but not at St Martin, Preston).

In 1944, the couple were living at 9 Council Cottages, Chequers Lane, Preston.

Bill and Mary had three children: Brian W Woodhams (born March 1939), John William (May 1944) and Michael David (November 1945).

In 1977, the writing was on the blackboard for Preston School which had been built in 1849 - and Mary was featured in a nostalgic news article:

'Three detached chalet houses may soon stand on the spot where Preston school children fidgeted on school benches – and for Mary Woodhams, who has been school cleaner for generations of them, it will mark the end of an era.

Mrs Woodhams' .... earliest memories of the school go back to when she was four. 'I wish I could come to the school as a child now,' she says, without a trace of fashionable nostalgia.

'These children are all happy together and there were no big boys to bully them.' There's no sentiment in her memories of cleaning at the old school either. The job which she took on from her mother, who had it since 1924, was a heavy dirty one.

She started cleaning in 1939. One of her duties was to empty the buckets which were the only form of toilets in the school in those days. Twice a week she had to dig holes to empty them into. Another duty was to fetch and chop firewood for the old-fashioned round stove that heated the 38 ft. by 20 ft. schoolhouse.

'I didn't mind the hard work – I liked it,' she said. 'After all, the school becomes part of you after all those years'.

Mary passed away in January 1984 and her husband, Bill, died three years later. Mary, Bill, Arthur and Harriet were all buried at St Martin, Preston.

(Left) Bill and Mary and *(top right, l to r)* Mike, John and Brian. *(Below)* The derelict school C. 1977

The Wallers - builders of Preston

Sir Edwin Lutyens has been lauded for the homes at Preston that he designed. But two generations of the Waller family left a legacy of homes in the village which is arguably greater than that of Lutyens'.

Bertram George Waller, or 'Bert' as he was known, was born in the village of Ickleford, near Hitchin, in the late autumn of 1907.

His family descended from the Wallers who built homes around Hitchin, beginning with the *Hornbeam Cottages* at Wymondley which were erected in around 1818 and sold for £40 each. Indeed, the building of houses was ingrained in the Waller family persona as their surname means, 'one who built walls around large estates'.

In 1928, Bert married Phyllis Powlter and the couple settled in Hitchin. They had three children: Peter George (who died, aged six weeks), Joan Margaret (born 1930) and Dennis Frederick (14 December 1931). In March 1939, the family moved into *Greenfields*, a bungalow at Back Lane, Preston which Bert built. (Bert's son, Dennis, later moved there and remodelled his home in 1975, as shown left. His family moved from *Greenfields* in 1980).

Soon after World War Two, Bert began his own construction business in 1946 as *B G Waller Ltd*. He built the houses along Butcher's Lane, together with some at Church Lane and Back Lane. His company also worked on other houses in the village and Princess Helena College.

In 1952, Bert was diagnosed with heart problems and was given just twelve months to live. He handed over the running of the business to Dennis and retired to Jaywick, near Clacton in Essex, as his doctors said he would benefit from the 'sea air'. The couple moved back to Preston in the early 1970's and lived in *Trebarwith*, Back Lane. They lived there until about 1980 when they moved to a house in Hitchin. Bert died in 1996 - he was 89 years old!

(Above) Some of the homes built by Wallers at Butchers Lane, Back Lane and Church Lane.

There was a news report that a 170-year-old tradition of Wallers building homes in the area was to end. The firm had employed fifty men, but these had been reduced to twelve – of whom nine had found alternative employment.

Dennis said, 'We're looking for an easier life - I've always fancied going into the holiday business. I've been building for thirty-six years and I wanted a change before I died. Once I'm dead and gone, I won't have another chance. I've been in the area all my life - my parents before me and my grandparents before them. It'll be like having my right arm chopped off'.

He calculated that he had worked on nearly every home in Preston over the years and a great many in Hitchin and the surrounding area including the Queen Mother's home at St Pauls Walden. Dennis added, 'The biggest satisfaction we've had is having a good crowd of working men around us'. Dennis didn't want to sell the business as a 'going concern' because they had built up a good reputation, so 'everything was auctioned'.

On 11 April 1955, Dennis (22), a carpenter and living at Newlands Lane, Hitchin, married Margaret Lilian Harper *(shown above)*. She was the daughter of the head game-keeper at Wain Wood and licensee of *The Chequers* at Preston, Frank Harper and his wife, Margaret. Dennis and Margaret had two children, Peter and Penny Waller.

Dennis continued to run the business and eventually bought the firm from his father, continuing to trade as B G Waller Ltd. His son, Peter, joined the firm in 1974. Peter worked in all the areas of building work and then worked in the office, with Frank Pugh. The business closed at the end of May, 1981.

Standing are Phyllis and Bert.
Seated, *l to r*: Margaret, Dennis and Joan (in 1988)

Then, during just eighteen years, three generations of Wallers died and were buried in St Martin's churchyard – Phyllis (3 April 1990), Bert (13 December 1996), Peter (8 October 1999) and Dennis (25 January 2008).

Nina Freebody - historian of Preston

Nina Freebody's parents, lived in the Leicestershire village of Sapcote. This community lies near Hinckley and between Nuneaton and Leicester. Nina Kate was born on 2 April 1919. She attended Hinkley Grammar School and then graduated at Leicester University, achieving a BA in history. This paved the way for a busy and productive life in local and general history.

In 1938, when she was 19, Nina married Robert Freebody *(the couple are shown right)* at Stockton-on-Tees in the north-east of England. They had four children. Nina taught at Leicester schools including the city's Collegiate Girls School about which she typically wrote a history. In 1967, Nina and Robert moved to *Red Roofs (shown right)*, a bungalow at Back Lane, Preston. Nina was appointed as Head of History at Collenswood School, Stevenage while Robert, a lecturer in Engineering, worked at Letchworth and Hatfield Poly-technic. It was while she was working at Stevenage that Nina studied for her MA degree. At some stage she also took an English Local History course.

Then, Nina retired from teaching in 1979. She passed away in January 1996, aged 76. Robert died in October of the following year Between 1971 and 1990, Nina's consuming fascination with local history inspired several articles in magazines such as, *Hertfordshire Countryside* and *Hertfordshire Past and Present*, the journal of the Hertfordshire Association for Local History.

The first of her pieces fittingly focused on the village she had made her home. It was entitled, **'A Typical Hertfordshire Village 100 Years Ago'** (1971). Twelve years later, in 1973, she wrote two further articles about the village featuring its public houses, **The Red Lion** and **The Chequers**. Some of these articles appeared in serial form in Preston's monthly newsletter. Spending her working life in Stevenage triggered a series of pieces about somewhat unusual and obscure aspects of the town's history:

'The Stevenage Giant' (1977)
'When the First Railway Train Passed through Stevenage in 1850' (1978)
'Schooling in Shephall: From the Eighteenth Century to the Coming of Stevenage New Town' (1980)
'Did the Exiled King of Portugal live in the Rookery? Some Interesting Residents of a Stevenage Home' (1982)
'Clocks and Clockmakers of Stevenage' (1983)
'The Throckmartins of Chesfield Manor' (1983)
'Brickyards and Brick-makers in Stevenage' (1990)

Nina's prolific pen also composed: **'Stories of the Broadwater Smithy: Fact and Fiction'** (1975); **'Home from Home: The Sue Ryder Home, Stagenhoe'** (1984); **'Industrial Archaeology in Schools'** (1974); **'Teaching Local History'** (1981); **'Leicester Collegiate Schools: Links with Hertfordshire'** (1980) and Hitchin's **Priory Gardens** (1981).

Along Preston's lanes, Nina found a soul-mate with a similar background and a passion for local history – Liz Hunter, of *Rose Cottage*.

Often Liz would return home to find, in her porch, notes or a photocopy of some data that an excited Nina had left thinking that Liz would find her research to be of interest. Liz remembers Nina as 'a humble academic with no arrogance; seeking no glory for herself'.

After retiring, Nina spent more time in her garden. In the 1980s, she entered the *Harkness Rose Competition* and won the second prize. Typically again, when interviewed she said that she was hoping to compile 'a major work on the gardens and nurserymen of Hertfordshire'. Although this tome was never written, Nina did produce an article for the Royal National Rose Society's magazine.

Until Mrs Maybrick produced a history *Scrapbook* of Preston in 1953, little had been written of Preston. From 1967, Nina eagerly shared the results of her research about the village which inspired and intrigued residents to want to know more.

Dick Middleditch - cricket umpire and gamekeeper

Dick was born Philip Dick Middleditch in July 1896 at Barningham, West Suffolk. He was the son of John (a farmer and carrier) and Elizabeth Middleditch. Dick left school before he was thirteen to train as a game keeper. When he was eighteen, Dick served with the Royal Artillery in Salonika, Greece during the First World War. After being demobbed, Dick married Ethel Margaret Meadows in the late autumn of 1924 in the Thetford Registration District, Norfolk. They settled at Loddon, Norfolk where the first two of their six children were born.

In 1929, Dick and his young family moved to *Keepers Cottage*, Dead Woman's Lane, Preston *(top right)* where the last four of their six children were born. Dick was employed until his retirement as a gamekeeper on the Kings Walden Estate. They later moved to *Bunyan's Cottage (right)* in Wain Wood.

Dick played cricket for Kings Walden but will be best remembered for his involvement with Preston Cricket Club for which he stood as umpire for forty-seven years from 1929 until 1976. He missed very few matches, except during the war years, when he served as a Corporal in the Home Guard. He was a Life Member and a Committee Member of the club and also prepared the pitches as the groundsman. It was a short climb for Dick through the woods from his home at *Bunyan's Cottage* to the Recreation Ground.

A cricketer said, 'His service to the club was absolutely unbelievable. He was always at his best on a cricket field and in the *Red Lion* afterwards'. Dick worked enjoyed a good relationship with Colonel Harrison of Kings Walden. 'Sometimes he was asked to load (guns) for his boss Col. Jack Harrison. They were friends as well as boss and game keeper.'

After his retirement, Dick and Ethel moved to 5 Holly Cottages, Back Lane. The homes had been built as tithe cottages for retired workers of long standing on the Kings Walden Estate. As well as his game-keeping duties, Dick was also a Special Constable for forty-one years. 'He enjoyed a pint at the *Red Lion*, a game of dominoes and darts with the lads from the village'.

Dick died on 4 January 1981 after being ill with cancer for some months. His coffin was driven around his game-keeping route on Sir Thomas Pilkington's estate before the funeral. A family wreath shaped like a cricket bat adorned the coffin and his ashes were sprinkled across the cricket ground. A clock was erected in his memory at the ground. Ethel continued to live at Holly Cottages until she moved to Mimsden Nursing Home at Hitchin where she died in 1994.

The reminiscences of Robert Sunderland

Three generations of Sunderlands lived at The Wilderness, Butchers Lane, Preston from 1934 until 1961:
Frank Thomas (1879 - 1956) and Lucy Kate Sunderland (1878 - 1961)
Edward Morris (1911 - 1989) and Olive Joan Sunderland (1918 - 1991)
and Edward and Olive's six children born between 1941 and 1957, who included Robert Sunderland.

Writes Robert Sunderland: My mother came to Preston to work as a Land Girl at *Castle Farm* in 1940. I believe she lodged with Mrs Worthington. She met my father (who was living with his parents at *The Wilderness*) and they married at St Martin.

There was a well in the cottage garden. It was rough, chalk-sided and about three feet in diameter. I remember it being 215 feet deep. Apparently, it was re-discovered in the late 1870s after the then owner/tenant stuck his pitchfork into the woodwork which covered it. My guess is that it was covered over after someone fell in many, many years earlier. Wells are very rare in Preston because it is a long way to dig for water and ponds are easier to create. The well may be very old, predating the cottage and may be a relic of nearby *Hunsden House, Preston Castle*. By the way, Butchers Lane is so called because *The Wilderness* was a butcher's shop, as evidenced by its high ceilings.

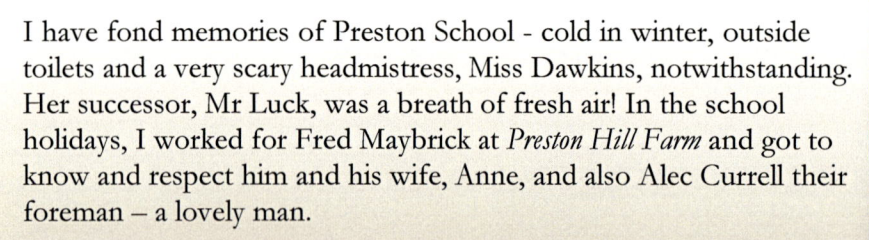

I have fond memories of Preston School - cold in winter, outside toilets and a very scary headmistress, Miss Dawkins, notwithstanding. Her successor, Mr Luck, was a breath of fresh air! In the school holidays, I worked for Fred Maybrick at *Preston Hill Farm* and got to know and respect him and his wife, Anne, and also Alec Currell their foreman – a lovely man.

Hill Farm had a wind pump - although Fred had disconnected the sails' drive and used a donkey engine in my time. When I worked for him in my youth, my weekly task was to start the engine and periodically check whether the tank was full. There was plenty of evidence of about six cottages which had been behind *Preston Hill Farm*. They are ploughed over now, as are the cottage ruins. There was also evidence of cottages below *Reeves Cottage* - all gone now.

(Above, from top down)
Frank Sunderland ;
Lucy Sunderland at *The Wilderness*;
Robert at *Preston Hill Farm*
and Hill Farm outbuildings.
(Left) The Wilderness (on right)
and *Rose Cottage* viewed from a *Pond Farm* field

There were at least seven ponds from Preston Green to the crossroads of Church Lane and Back Lane/ Butchers Lane. The pond at that corner was excavated for the sewage pumping station in 1969. All the rest were filled in during the house building programme of the 1950's/1960's. I'm pleased to see the village pond is back. There were also two ponds at *Pond Farm*, but both are now gone and a pond at *Preston Hill Farm* – also gone. All were dew ponds and are a sad loss to our environment.

I remember visiting the site of *Offley Holes House* when I was a boy and poking about in the still-visible ruins. Some interesting 'treasures' there, such as spent .303 cartridges (I can't recall if they had been fired or whether they simply went bang in the fire); the steel heel-piece from an army boot and bits of barbed wire. The outline of the House's foundations were still clear in the early 1950's, but they are far too overgrown to see anything now - although some of the shrubs may survive. I was always under the impression that the House had been built on much older foundations. The coach-house is still extant and inhabited. It was occupied by Mrs Fountain in the 1960s - she kept the Preston village shop after Rose Stanley gave it up.

Concerning Welei or Wayley which is located a only few hundred metres away from Offley Holes. It is a strange and somewhat eerie place - much feared when I was young. I imagine it fell victim to the Black Death. Many hamlets did in Hertfordshire. There were probably more dwellings at Sootfield Green too. It was known sixty years ago as Pilgrim's Plot - which may be a reference to reference to Bunyan. Its 'green-at-the-lanes' crossing was a favourite stopping place for gypsies - proper ones, true Roma, with their hooped, horse-drawn caravans. They would call to sell pegs and 'lucky heather' but would never venture inside the dwelling of a 'gorgio'.

Looking at old photographs of Preston, there is no doubt it was a much more attractive village than the clean, sanitized and up-market place we see today! (Although the living conditions would have been pretty grim.) Derek Seebohm bought *The Wilderness* and the land from my grandparents in 1956. The deal was that my grandparents could live there rent-free for the remainder of their lives and that he would build *Chequers Cottage* at the other end of the field. This was erected in 1958. In the event, *The Wilderness* did not come onto the market until late 1963. I wanted to buy it but my fiancee would have none of living in a damp, draughty cottage with no hot water, no inside 'loo' (even the attraction of a rare, outside 'two holer' couldn't move her!).

In 1967, we returned to Preston and built *Thurlaston* on Church Lane. Our children were born there. I don't live in Preston today - being a Little Wymondley resident - but I am *of* Preston and it will always be my home. I inherited Frank Pugh's shares in the *Red Lion,* so I can be found there once or twice a week.

Lucy Sunderland in the living room of *The Wilderness; Preston Hill Farm*

Samuel Hall and family

Samuel Hall and his family moved to Preston in 1915. He was landlord of the Red Lion until 1920 and he remained in the village until his death in 1940. His is a story tinged with disappointment and sadness.

Samuel Hall was born at Paddington, West London in 1869 and married Lily Woods at Kilburn, London on 19 August 1896. When he married, Samuel described his occupation as a clerk but five years later, he was a company manager - he was employed by a Swedish match manufacturer and importer. Samuel and Lily already had five children: Elsie Lily (born, 1897); Leonard Samuel (1900); the twins, Dorothy and Sidney (1905) and Cecil (1911).

The family were living at Willsden, London. But Samuel lost his job and found himself at Preston as the landlord of the *Red Lion* in March, 1915. The two oldest children, Elsie and Leonard, stayed in London while Dorothy, Sidney and Cecil began attending Preston School in 1915.

Seated are Samuel and Lily Hall; standing are Dorothy and Sidney; in the foreground is Cecil. Lily is also pictured above, right.

Samuel worked at the *Red Lion* for five years until around 1920. Then, by 1925, his family were living in a newly-built council house on the north side of Chequers Lane *(see far right)*. Cecil, now aged 16, worked as a dairyman's assistant at Temple Dinsley. One of the boys went on to work for the Seebohms at Poynders End.

The charming postcard of Preston Well c.1920 *(right, and which is on the front cover of this book)* was sent by Dorothy to her sister Elsie. On the back she wrote, 'Elsie, puzzle, find Cecil, love Dolly.' Is Cecil the boy *(shown second right)*?

About this time, Lily was admitted to the Three Counties Asylum at Arlesey, Beds. One Saturday afternoon, 26 August 1926, Dorothy cycled the six miles to Arlesey to visit her mother and on the return journey, on the hill between Letchworth and Hitchin, she collided with a car.

Dorothy *(above)* was severely injured sustaining a broken neck and shoulder blade and several fractures to other limbs. Although hospitalised for almost six weeks, she never recovered and was buried in St Martin's churchyard on 5 October 1926. Dorothy was just twenty years old. Her death 'shocked the village'.

Samuel, without Lily and Dorothy for company, was living with his son, Cecil *(shown above)*. Cecil went into service, possibly with the Pilkingtons at Kings Walden but he did not stay in Preston - in the 1930s he became a footman at Hatchford Park, near Cobham, Surrey. Samuel was now alone at Preston. He eked out a living, delivering newspapers around the village and passed away in 1940. Sidney (having been alerted by a neighbour, Mrs Crawley) travelled back to Preston with his wife despite the deep snow that forced them to abandon the bus near the bottom of Preston Hill. He found Samuel's home a little neglected - full bottles of milk stood on the stairs and a dead crow was on top of a wardrobe.

Samuel was buried at St Martin on 17 January 1940, aged 70. Even today, he is remembered: 'He used to talk to everyone in the village'. He cycled in all weathers and had little in the way of home comforts. Lily Hall died at Arlesey in 1950.

The Scott family of Church Lane

The Scott family lived at Preston for more than a century - from the 1820s until the death of Will Scott in 1930. The bread winners were farm workers and they lived most, if not all, of this time in Rose Cottage which was next door to and to the right of Bunyan's Chapel.

The Scotts originally lived in Hertford until Thomas Scott (1758 - 1812) and his wife Lydia moved to Peters Green, Kimpton. They not only owned their cottage there, but in his will Thomas described himself as a yeoman - a cut above a farm worker. However, his estate was eventually distributed between their nine children and so became diluted.

A younger son, James, an agricultural labourer, moved to Preston, probably soon after marrying local girl, Mary Ann Joyner, at Kings Walden in 1824. The couple also had nine children and appear to have rented *Rose Cottage* (which was to the right of *Bunyan's Chapel*) from Dinah Swain. The cottage had been earlier rented by Mary Ann's father, William Joyner. James (aged 64) died in 1862 and was buried at St John's Road, Hitchin where Mary Ann (70) was also laid to rest in 1876.

A son, William Scott, was born at Preston and baptised on 14 November 1834 at Hitchin. He married Emma Bushell on 22 December 1877. William *(below left, aged 93)* and Emma *(below right)* continued living in *Rose Cottage*. William was a farm worker and Emma took in laundry.

Remembering that William was forty-three when he married, it is hardly surprising that the couple had but two children, a daughter Mary Ellen who was born towards the end of 1878 and Esther Susan, born April 1882, but died 17 March 1884. The family line continued through Mary Ellen's son, Harold Scott. William (1930), Emma (1924), and Mary Ellen (now Herron) (1953) were all buried in St Martin's churchyard.

Harold Scott's memories: 'I was born in 1906 in the village of Preston. I lived in a little cottage called *Rose Cottage*, which faced the side of the *Bunyan's Chapel*. The cottage was of clapboard construction and had a barn attached to one side, with a bedroom built over the barn. My mother was Mary Ellen. She worked in the Hitchin Grammar School as the Matron while I was young and drove into Hitchin in a pony and trap. She was involved with the *Bunyan's Chapel*, possibly as an organist. *(I recall)* collecting water from the village pump on the green, even after mains water was piped to the houses, because people were suspicious of piped water; having to get milk from one of the local farms by walking across a field; of the two public houses in the village, *The Chequers* was a bit of a rough pub; Mr (RDV) Pryor used to walk round the village in a tweed jacket and plus-fours; an Army Artillery unit with despatch riders that camped in a field outside the village, laid Field Telegraph lines and carried out manoeuvres, probably in 1913/14.'

Harold Scott's photographs of Preston in the 1950s: *(top) Bunyan's Chapel* and the *Red Lion* and *(bottom)* St Martin's churchyard

The Armstrong family

Frederick Armstrong was from farming stock. He was born in 1839 at Lower Stondon, Beds, the son of William and Phoebe Armstrong. In 1871, William kept the 232-acre *Blake Farm* in Great Wymondley, near Hitchin. On 3 December 1873, Frederick married Emma Kirkby at Ware, Herts. Although Emma was born at Hatfield Broad Oak, Essex in 1844, she was no stranger to Preston. Her parents, Samuel and Dorothy Kirkby, had farmed at *Castle Farm*, Preston since about 1850. Soon after their marriage, Frederick *(shown below)* took over the tenancy of *Preston Hill Farm* in the parish of Kings Walden. The couple had seven children.

Frederick was a prime mover in the building of St Martin's Church at Preston. He organised a musical soiree which raised £11 towards the Church Fund. He also enjoyed a good reputation in agricultural circles. In May 1910, a dinner was held on his seventieth birthday at the Angel Hotel, Hitchin when he was presented with a life-sized portrait of himself which had been paid for by 125 subscribers. When Frederick died of cancer in April 1911, he was described as a familiar and popular figure at Hitchin market. His estate was valued at £2,037. He and Emma (in 1929) were buried at St Martin.

A newspaper tribute to Frederick noted that he was 'one of the most prominent and best known agriculturists in the Hitchin district. Of a genial and open-hearted nature, Mr Armstrong had hosts of friends in the the neighbourhood. In his early years (he) was a member of the Herts. Yeomanry...(and was) a staunch conservative of the old school and a strong churchman'

Two of Frederick's sons: *(left)* Frederick William and Thomas George Armstrong

Thomas and another son, Henry James owned property at *Chequers Cottages* - their homes were like bookends of the row: No 1, Thomas and No 6 *(nearest right, below)*, Henry.

There is evidence that Thomas owned his cottage from 1918 and he appears to have rented it out. Then, in 1946, Thomas (who was living at *Crossways*, Hitchin Hill, Hitchin) sold the property to William Wheeler of *The Garage*, Kings Walden for £500. Its tenant was probably Preston's policeman at the time.

Henry James (Jack) Armstrong with his wife, Gertrude Kate Wilkins

Henry (Jack) Armstrong married Gertrude Kate Wilkins (born in 1880 at Tottenham, East London, the daughter of a commercial traveller in tea) in 1918. He bought 6 *Chequers Cottages* for £300 using money inherited from his father. The couple lived there for the rest of their lives. Jack (78) died in January 1962, aged 78; Gertrude (83), in June 1964. Both were buried at St Martin, Preston. They had one daughter, Eileen.

A charming study of Eileen in Wain Wood

Eileen married Leonard Thomas 'Lenny' Newell at St Martin on 4 December 1940. Lenny was born in February 1911 at the village of Ombersham, near Midhurst, Sussex. He was the only child of a carter on a farm. After his father's death while fighting in The Great War and his mother's re-marriage, Lenny (16) boarded *Montrose* at Liverpool in March 1927 along with 86 other boys aged between 14 and 16 from orphanage and Dr Barnado's Homes. Their destination was Canada. After working there for around six years, he returned to Britain and worked as a farm labourer for Colonel Harrison on the Kings Walden Estate. This was how the couple met.

Like many couples of the day, Lenny and Eileen lived with their in-laws - in this case, Eileen's parents at 6 *Chequers Cottages*. Their home was now known as *Elm Cottage*. The property doubled as Preston's Post Office and local letters were delivered by Eileen, who was described as a Post Office worker when she married. Their home was the village Post Office until 1947/8.

The couple had four children: Christopher James, Malcolm, Stephen and Barbara Elizabeth Newell. Lenny continued to work as a farm labourer at various farms in the village - *Ladygrove Farm, Preston Hill Farm* and *Castle Farm*. He then worked in shops at Hitchin. A stint with BG Wallers, builders at Preston, was next. When he retired, Lenny was working at the Highways Department Yard off the Hitchin Road at Preston. Lenny died in early 1982. Soon afterwards, Eileen moved to Passingham Avenue, Hitchin and then to *Woodlands View Home* at Stevenage, where she died in 2010.

As Lenny and Eileen lived next door to my family, I have a clear memory of the Newells. My impression of Lenny was that he was a quiet, rather withdrawn man and that Eileen was a bubbly, effervescent woman who loved life. Their son, Chris agreed, adding that his mother was 'lively'. She enjoyed dancing and played tennis at Preston's Recreation Ground. Like most villagers, they tended their garden and rarely bought vegetables. They were stored near the cool water tank that was at the rear of the *Chequers Cottages* gardens. Eileen would often walk to Hitchin with a pram to shop for the family. Although the Newells have left Preston, Chris Newell played cricket for one of the village teams (belying his seventy-plus years!) and on weekends can often be found in *The Red Lion*.

(Above, l to r) Thomas Armstrong, Lenny, Eileen, Rosemary Kay and Jack Armstrong. *(Right)* Barbara and Eileen Newell and Gertrude Armstrong

Alfred and Emily Wray

If ever a family crest were created for the Wrays of Hertfordshire, it would feature a hurdle and a bill hook. They were hurdle-makers. Six generations and sixteen Wray men have been found who worked at this craft. The pros and cons of this employment: as specialist artisans, they earned a little more than the ubiquitous 'Ag Lab', but as demand was limited, sons of hurdle-makers had to move from home to find work. So the Wrays roamed around the Hertfordshire parishes between Hatfield and Hertford. Alfred's father, Charles Wray, was born in Tewin, moved to Hill End, near Preston and thence to Austage End, where he died.

Alfred was born at the nearby village of Charlton on 16 April 1858. When he was seven, he belatedly began attending Breachwood Green school. The school log book noted that he was 'rather backward for his age'. By 1871, Alfred was already working as a ploughboy - at the age of twelve.

Emily Currell was born at Preston on 22 December 1863, the first daughter of the unmarried Thomas Currell and Mary Fairey. Eight years later, in 1871, her family was living at Gosmore (which is between Preston and Hitchin). From an early age, Emily plaited straw like the majority of the local girls.

By 1881, the Currells had moved to Back Lane, Preston and Alfred was still living at Austage End. The next year, in March 1882, the pair were involved in a court case. The newspaper report gives an insight into their lives. Emily worked at *The Bull* at Gosmore and was called 'my *little* girl' by the wife of the inn-keeper - she was a slight figure even later in life. Alfred (who was now described as a 'hurdle-maker') was having his lunch and beer at eleven o'clock in the pub. That the two were together here was surely no mere coincidence.

Seven months later, Alfred and Emily married at St Mary's Church, Hitchin on 11 November 1882. Both were uneducated and illiterate - they marked the register instead of signing their names. Neither of them noticed that Alfred's surname had been misspelt as 'Ray'.

The first of Alfred and Emily's fourteen children, Arthur, was born in February, 1883. Their children were healthy - 'all born and lived well'. In 1891, the couple and five children lived in a two-roomed house at Back Lane, next door to Emily's mother, Mary Currell. Their home was immediately to the north of the footpath that still leads to The Green. They moved to Poynders End briefly in 1897, but by 1898 they had returned to Back Lane and were paying 4/5d (22p) rent a week to their landlord, GIE Pryor. Three years later, in 1901, the family had moved to another tumbledown cottage on the north side of Chequers Lane. In 1914, they crossed the lane and were living in the Lutyens-designed, newly-built 5 *Chequers Cottages (below, second from end)*.

96

After the succession of squalid, run-down and insanitary hovels to which they were accustomed, their new home must have seemed like a palace. They had a scullery, a living room and four bedrooms (there were now seven children at home) and an attached w.c. They had a long garden for their vegetable and chickens and even a pungent, earthy-smelling barn in which to store their produce. Attached to the barn was a water pump connected to an underground tank which stored rain water.

c. 1935

Emily's attitude towards her children's education seems to have varied according to the circumstances and needs of her family. For example, her daughter, Carrie (12), was 'kept at home to plait' and left school early to 'help her mother'. Similarly, another daughter, Alice (11), was 'frequently kept at home to mind babies and was backward in consequence' - at the time there were three children aged three and under in the household. The children were dispatched to school as soon as possible - it was a supervised haven and gave Emily time and space for her work at home.

Of the boys, Ernest (who had earlier played truant - 'a rare fault in this school') left school, aged twelve, to go to work. Yet, Jack Wray received a watch for five years perfect attendance. In February, 1891 all the Ray (sic) children were sent home for their 'school pence' as six weeks 'pence' was owed – a sign of either their parent's poverty or indifference to education.

It was perhaps ironic that in February 1920, Emily started work as the school cleaner for wages of £1 a month - only to resign her post in the following November. Possibly the need to work was forced upon her. For some years, Alfred followed in his family's tradition and worked as a hurdle-maker - "'e laid 'edges lovely". He was self-employed and travelled from farm-to-farm. However, while working in the woods of the Temple Dinsley estate, Alfred lost a limb. He had been felling trees using a block and tackle when a pulley wound around his leg.

As a result of this horrific accident, the family was allowed to live rent-free in their cottage by Mr. Vickers - which helped to 'make ends meet'. Later, when their daughter Flossie heard that the cottage could be purchased, she immediately visited Mr Vickers and the deal was made.

(Left) the rear of 5 *Chequers Cottages* and its barn.
(Above) Alfred Wray

Like many of the women in the village, Emily worked in service at Temple Dinsley. This environment influenced the way in which she organized her own household. She 'was very strict' and 'a stickler for doing things properly'. Before every meal the children had to wash at the well.

Life was hard for Emily with so many children for whom to care. She would regularly walk the three miles to Hitchin on Tuesdays and Saturdays for the family's shopping. The last haul up Preston Hill burdened down with groceries must have been exhausting! She also walked to Hitchin for the straw which she plaited and to sell the finished product. In the summertime, she might be found in the fields, often with her children, as she picked stones and gleaned corn. She occasionally carried a bundle of straw home balanced on her head.

(L to r) Emily, her sister, Phyllis Jenkins, and Annie Peters

Emily had 'some queer ways'. She was superstitious and insisted knives and forks were uncrossed when laid on the table. Her children were told 'not to go up Green Lane as there were witches there'. The playing of tennis by the children was forbidden during the times of church services and on Sundays there was no knitting or sewing of buttons as it was the Sabbath.

Later in life, Emily 'broke her hip and never had it fixed'. Her son, Sam, made her a crutch from an upended broom which he padded for comfort. She was known affectionately as 'granny with the broom'.

Alfred died on 28 April 1934 aged sixty-six. The causes of his death were senile decay, syncope and gangrene of the foot due to diabetes. It is thought that some dye from a sock infected his foot when he was tending a wind pump at the bottom of the garden. Four days later, Alfred was buried at St Martin's Church.

Emily now was living with her children, Flossie, Nan and Sam for company. In later years she wore a black dress, sometimes with a black and white apron and sat in a rocking chair in the corner of the room.

Her hair was 'scrunched back in a bun'. She would say 'if you can see a cobweb you can get up there and lick it down'.

On 10 March 1951, Emily died. She was eighty-seven years old. She had suffered with diabetes ('the sugar') and she died from heart failure and arteriosclerosis which is a thickening of the arteries caused by cholesterol plaque.

Emily was buried five days later at St Martin's Church. Her unmarked grave is near the door of the church.

Emily certainly had a hard life bringing up so many children and with a husband who could be difficult at times. From her photographs she looks worn but has a ready smile. She regularly enjoyed 'her half of stout at *The Chequers*'. A granddaughter remembers her fondly as a 'real granny…kindly, giving and a good listener'.

Alf and Em were typical of many rural Hertfordshire families of the time. He toiled hard on the land from his youth and she supplemented his meagre wage - mainly by 'the Plait' - and cared for her household. Their story truly is 'an everyday story of country folk'.

William (Bill) and Rose Stanley

This account begins with Frederick Robinson, a master tailor living at *Vine Cottage*, Preston Green from the late 1870s. One of his daughters, Margaret Elizabeth Robinson, married Harry Worthington, an engine driver from Dymock, Gloucestershire at St Martin on Christmas Day, 1909. The couple lived at Vine Cottage, Preston Green. A little more than a year later, Rose Margaret Irene Worthington was born on 31 December 1910.

By the late 1920s, Harry and Margaret Worthington were also living at *Vine Cottage*. In the summer of 1947, Rose Worthington married William (Bill) Vincent Stanley (born 7 March 1913) in the Hitchin registration district and by the 1950s the Stanleys (who had one son, born in 1950) were living with Rose's parents at *Vine Cottage*.

Harry (1950) and Margaret (1959) died and were buried at St Martin. Meanwhile, Bill and Rose Stanley (who ran the adjacent village shop *(right)* for a time) continued to live at *Vine Cottage*.

Bill *(right and below)* was buried at St Martin in 1993 and Rose's *(right)* ashes were scattered in the graveyard after her death in early 1997.

Mrs Ann Maybrick

(Frances Edith) Ann Maybrick, nee Jamieson, was born in 1911 at Morpeth, Northumberland. She married Frederick ('Freddie') Hinings Maybrick (born 1903 at Prescott, Lancs.) at Kensington, London in late 1942. The couple had no children and farmed at *Preston Hill Farm*. When they retired they moved to one of the farm's labourers' cottages and re-christened it, *Reeves Cottage (see page 64)*. Freddie died in 1987, and Ann in 1989.

When writing the history of Preston was just a twinkle in one's eye, I mooted the idea to two Preston ladies. Somewhat sniffily, the reaction was, 'Why would you want to do that – it's already been done'. And she was right. Ann Maybrick lovingly compiled a scrapbook history of the village in 1953.

A newspaper reported, "Ann was asked to produce the book for a competition held by the WI to mark the Coronation – and was very surprised at the time when it beat all the other Hertfordshire entries!

"Since then, the book has become a treasured possession in Preston. It has been in such demand that four copies have been made and the villagers take it in turns to look after the original.

"'It is enormously popular', admits Mrs Maybrick, 'It has been round and round the village'. This isn't surprising, since the work is a readable and fascinating account of Preston and Langley village life from Domesday times until 1953. It uses paintings and drawings done by people in the villages, old maps carefully copied by Mrs Maybrick and old photos.

"It's beautifully bound with leather from Russell's tan yards in Hitchin – and an inscription records the fact that Russell's also supplied the leather used to bind the Queen's Coronation prayer-book and Bible. 'I went to see Mr Percy Russell and asked him for some leather', recalls Mrs Maybrick. 'He said I could pay him later – and he never sent us the bill'.

"Mrs Maybrick started writing and compiling the book during the Second World War. 'I used to sit in the old village farm office by the phone on fire watch,' she said. 'There were always several people with me who had lived in the village and I used to pick their brains for information.

"Compiling the book also meant trips to St Mary's Church in Hitchin where Mrs Maybrick would spend hours in a 'little dusty room' looking through Parish records.

"Some of the photos in the book are old postcards copied at *Andrew's Chemists* in Brand Street, Hitchin and others were taken later.

"Records like these are supremely important to a village like Preston where many of the older people find that village life is declining." *(N Herts. Gazette, 23/8/1979)*

Ann's scrapbook is reproduced in its entirety on the Preston History web site, including its crocheted cover and the watercolours of birds shown above.

The Peters family

The Peters were one of the most prominent families in Preston in the nineteenth century. Yet, in 1800, there were no Peters living in Preston.

During the late 1700s, the Peters family was at Whitwell in the parish of St Pauls Walden. Joseph and Martha Peters married at St Pauls Walden (20 December 1795) and had eight children baptised there between 1799 - 1811. Many of the family then moved the short distance to Kings Walden where the couple died in the late 1830s.

Judging by the occupations of Joseph's six sons, they were a 'cut above' the ubiquitous agricultural labourers. Four were shoemakers and another was a baker.

Perhaps there were just too many shoemakers in Kings Walden, for Joseph Peters jnr (born 1804) moved to Preston to ply his cordwaining trade there when he was about 21 years old.

He features in the 1825 Valuation for the Poor Law in Preston which also helpfully provides a reference to his shop at Preston Green - indeed he was to live and trade from these thatched premises *(shown below)* for almost 60 years until his death.

Four years after arriving in Preston, Joseph married Sarah Joyner. Joseph and Sarah had 13 children between 1830 and 1852 including three who died young and who were buried at Kings Walden. The surviving children married Preston people including members of the Palmer, Jeeves, Sharp, Andrews and Payne families.

The Peters boys did not follow in the family trade as shoemakers. All were described as 'ag labs' in the 1871 census, but two seem to have specialized in caring for horses - William (groom) and Samuel (horse keeper). Most stayed in Preston for a time - Joseph (Blacksmiths Road), Samuel (Church Lane), Peter and Elijah (The Green), and Thomas (Back Lane). Towards the end of the century, some had joined the drift away from Preston - William was at Kings Walden and Samuel was in Little Almshoe.

By 1884, Sarah had established a plaiting school for village children at their home.

The patriarch, Joseph Peters, died in October 1883. Sarah then lived with her married daughter, Mary Sharp, at Chequers Lane until her death in May 1891. Joseph and Sarah had no fewer than 45 grandchildren and in 1901, there were 21 people in Preston with the Peters surname.

(Left) Bertha Peters (born 1878) daughter of Joseph and Sarah. She was a Preston School monitor from July 1891 until at least 1901. In 1897 it was said of her, 'Bertha Peters has had to take the infants entirely. She is a good help" and she "has kept the infants very fairly up with their work'.

In the middle of the twentieth century, there were still Peters at Preston. Joseph and Sarah's grandchildren, Annie Christobel (who was RDV Pryor's housekeeper until his death in 1945) was living at *Laburnum Lodge*, Preston Green; Annie Margaret (Nance) was at 2 Chequers Cottages and Walter Charles was residing at 6 *Holly Cottages*, Back Lane.

Joseph and Sarah's great grandson, Walter Charles and his wife, Queenie, were living at 15 Chequers Lane and James, Hubert and Eliza Peters were at Hitchwood.

One of the noticeably unusual features of the Peters family in the late nineteenth century was their choice of Christian names. The list includes Minnie Euphemia, Florence Georgina, Gilbert Henry, Annie Christobel, Leonard Charles, Agnes Louisa, Amy Priscilla and Edith Lucy.

At a time when single Christian names were still the norm and names such as Thomas, John, Mary and Elizabeth proliferated, such a variety of names is a refreshing change for the local historian.

However, in 2004, after more than 150 years of a Peters' presence in Preston, once again the name does not appear in local records.

A Peters portrait gallery

(Above) Samuel (a horse keeper) and Henrietta (nee Palmer) Peters who were both born at Preston in the summer of 1846 and who married at St Mary, Hitchin in 1872. They lived for more than 20 years at Church Lane, Preston until their move to Little Almshoe, Herts. in July 1896.

(Above, left) Arthur Peters (1875 - 1915) who married Alice Peters (dau. of William and Mary) in 1908 at Hitchin. *(Above, right)* Albert Charles Peters (1881 - 1974) who was head gardener at Kingshott School, Ippollitts. His medal celebrates 50 years in horticulture.

(Above) In the centre are Thomas (bn 1853) and Martha (nee Andrews, bn 1856) Peters probably with their fourteen children. They married at St Mary, Hitchin on 18 September 1875. After their marriage, Thomas and Martha lived at Back Lane until the 1890s when they moved to Preston Green. Annie ('Nance') Peters is front centre. She was a spinster and lived at 2 *Chequers Cottages* until her death in 1982. The two men at either end of the back row are the twins Edward (left) and Reginald Peters. Agnes Peters is second left, middle row. The photograph was probably taken in the early 1920's.

Tom Ashton - baker of Preston

Tom Ashton was the baker in Preston from the mid-1880s until 1934. Born in 1856, Tom was the son of master baker James Ashton and Elizabeth. He was raised in the Bedfordshire village of Shillington where, aged 14, he helped his father in the bakery.

In 1878, Tom (21) married Catherine (Kate) Smith (21) at Shillington. They arrived in Preston in the late 1880s. The couple had eight children.

They put down their roots at *The Old Forge*, Church Lane *(right)* which was almost opposite the lych-gate of St Martin. This was a convenient location for Tom as he was the organist at the church. If Tom thought the sermon was dragging, he would look at his watch and glance meaningfully at the vicar.

Tom's 'delicious rock cakes' were supplied for the cricketers afternoon teas. Villagers such as Maggie Wray delivered Tom's bread and cakes by bicycle and Reginald Peters was a bakery helper in 1901.

Like many of the tradesmen in Preston, Tom had his own means of transport - a pony and trap - which he used to collect supplies and deliver his delicacies.

Discovering what 'made things tick' was a passion for Tom. He liked clocks and delighted in repairing them. *The Old Forge* resounded not with the sound of a blacksmith's hammer but with a cacophony of chimes from the many clocks which festooned its walls. Tom also made a crystal radio set from a kit. He would listen to broadcasts of classical music and, as he was able to read music, he would follow recitals using his own score.

Clearly Tom was one of Preston's familiar figures. On one occasion he organized a charabanc trip for the villagers to watch the Derby at Epsom. Tom was the enumerator at Preston when the 1911 Census was taken. Perhaps not quite so well appreciated by the locals was his work as rating officer for Preston. At the Preston parish meeting of March 1895, Tom was appointed 'overseer'.

Catherine died in 1926. Tom was in constant pain from a hernia. He died in 1934. They are buried in a double grave in St Martin's churchyard.

The marriage of Mary Elizabeth Ashton to Sidney R Skinner in 1926. This photograph was taken outside *The Old Forge*, Preston. *Front row, l to r:* ?,?,?,?, Sidney R Skinner (groom), Mary Elizabeth Ashton (bride), ?, Catherine (Kate) Ashton, Tom Ashton.

Flossie/Florrie Sugden (nee Wray)

Although we knew her as 'Auntie Flossie', her parents named her 'Florrie'. She was born on 15 August 1889 at Back Lane, Preston and was eventually baptized on 12 July 1891.

She began attending school very early - on the 25 April 1892 - indeed the headmistress commented that 'Florence Wray is young for Standard Three', in 1898. Her school record is only noteworthy because she was knocked down and injured in the playground by Herbert Robinson (the son of Preston's tailor) in 1899 and was later absent for ten days in the summer of 1902 with 'a gathering in her head'.

In 1911, Flossie was at Bracknell, London where she was cooking for an architect and his family.

Was it her London connections that smoothed the way for Flossie to become a nurse? Certainly, her acceptance by the nursing profession shows some resourcefulness. The nursing service in those times was 'incredibly concerned with social class and status'. They gave preference to daughters of professional people such as teachers, chaplains and Army officers. The following are typical comments in the minutes of the Nursing Board:

'Not in the least acceptable; her father is a shoemaker.'
'Not a lady by birth nor by education.'
'Hardly up to standard, personally and socially.'

Quite how Flossie 'got through this social net' and later married above her station (as we shall see) is a mystery. However, sometime in 1919, this thirty-year-old nurse from Preston sailed for five weeks to India through the Suez Canal and then travelled a further two days across the Indian sub-continent to the dust and heat of the North West Frontier. She received a medal (right) for her service at Waziristan from 1919-21.

A niece remembers being spellbound by Flossie's stories of her Indian experiences – of panthers who carried off small animals from the camp at night.

In 1921, there was an announcement in *Pioneer Mail and India Weekly News*: "A marriage has been arranged and will shortly take place between Miss F Wray of Preston, and Captain H Sugden IAR".

This was a bombshell. Harold Sugden's grandfather was a surgeon and an apothecary. His father was a clergyman and architect who designed several Scottish churches. Harold was commissioned to the Indian Army on 4 September 1918 and became a temporary Captain in 1920 until October 1922. They married at St Thomas' Church, Dera Ismail Khan, diocese of Lahore, Pakistan on 14 April 1921.

But the marriage was doomed. It is generally believed by Flossie's family that it foundered because of pressure from Harold's relatives. That she kept her engagement ring and passed it on to a favourite niece perhaps shows her feelings about her marriage.

When she returned to her parents' home at Preston, she became a matron at 'Foxholes' maternity home in Hitchin which is a measure of her ability and strong (not to say stern) character. She was known as 'Matron Sugden' and was nursing there in 1951 when her mother died. She would drive there somewhat erratically. Flossie then worked in a home for the elderly at Stevenage.

As soon as she heard that 5 *Chequers Cottages* could be bought, she visited the owner, Mr. Vickers, and purchased it.

Towards the end of her life, Flossie became a little unbalanced. She locked her sister, Nan, out of the house and a villager remembers being terrified at school because Flossie arrived there declaring that there was a terrible epidemic and demanding that all the children had to be inoculated. Flossie died intestate in 1966 at Fairfield Mental Hospital, Stotfold, Beds. Her sister Nan Wray continued to live at the family home until her death in 1978. It was then sold for £18,000.

Flossie would glare at me and bristle with trembling lips during the most trivial of chats. She is shown above with a cherubic, well-behaved nephew in 1951. I only wish I could remember the occasion.

This book is dedicated to the memory of my parents: Sam and Grace (nee Mills) Wray

Mum and Dad could hardly have come from more disparate backgrounds but they met at Preston because of two factors: the Second World War and my mother's deafness.

All of Dad's known ancestors lived within seventeen miles of Preston and were agricultural workers - *all* of them! My maternal forefathers were a completely different kettle of fish. They include sailors (one was a powder monkey at *Trafalgar*), the 'oldest and most intimate friend' of John Pounds (the originator of the *Ragged School* movement), London silversmiths and boat-builders, and land owners/farmers at Oakham and Hampshire. My maternal great grandfather was a councillor who owned a string of shops at Stoke Newington, London and his daughters (my great aunts) married men who were knighted and awarded the CBE. My maternal grandparents met while students at Hartley College (which became Southampton University) and my great uncle was Headmaster of Portsmouth's Beneficial School. Grandpa was also a teacher. This was quite a contrast to my father who according to the Preston School Log left school three months shy of his fourteenth birthday to help with the harvest, barely able to read or write.

When Mum was twenty-one, she became profoundly deaf. Shortly afterwards she moved to London, ostensibly to care for her widowed grandmother, but found time to enjoy the attractions of society in the capital - The Proms, Lyons Corner House and so on. She drove around the metropolis in a car. When the Second World War erupted in her own words, 'you see, the war came along and it meant that you had to do your bit. The forces wouldn't take me as I jolly well couldn't hear so the only other alternative was the Land Army'. Mum signed up as Land Girl No 37,296 on 25 January 1941 and was sent to *Ladygrove Farm*, Preston.

(Above) Dad in a familiar slouch at *Preston Hill Farm* - the tractor driver is Reg Darton. *(Right)* Mum driving a tractor at *Ladygrove Farm*.

She (32) and Dad (39) married at Portsmouth on 17 March 1945. At the time, Dad was working for Mr Maybrick at *Preston Hill Farm* and eventually Mum and Dad made a home at what is now *Reeves Cottage*. After the life style to which she was accustomed, to be isolated so far from other villagers (never mind her family) must have been hard to accept. Several people have said they told Dad, 'It's not the right place for her...you've got no business taking her there' or words to that effect. She escaped when their children were born. Our little family moved in with my now widowed grandfather at Portsmouth. About twelve years later, Mum had an operation to remove the stirrup bone from her ear - and her hearing was restored!

I loved Dad and Mum for totally different reasons and like all of us I am very aware of inheriting my parents and my ancestors traits, good and bad. My regret is that I will not see their reactions when seeing this book - though I know Dad would only look at the photographs - and maybe sniff!

News stories and Preston

The value of news stories when researching local history has already been commented on. They provide illuminating details of village life. For example, the present-day Castle Farmhouse is obviously no ancient pile, but when and why was it built? In August 1868, a 'Great Destruction of Farm Produce' was reported. A fire which raged during the whole of one Saturday consumed 'every vestige of the farm buildings...except a small granary'. Fortunately, the owner, Mrs Curling, was insured with the Royal Exchange. And so, Phoenix-like, a new farm house must thereafter have risen from the ashes.

In July 1928, there was a celebration of Bunyan's ministry at Bunyan's Dell in Wain Wood. Five hundred folk assembled there and photographs were taken and survive (see below).

It is a newspaper that added an intriguing fact: Hitchin historian, Reginald Hine, was the chairman. Is that Hine addressing the crowd in the photo? Only the news account places him at the scene.

News reports also add to our knowledge bank about Preston residents and maybe our ancestors. In March 1860, my great grandfather, Charles Wray (hurdle-maker), violently assaulted another hurdle-maker after accusing him of 'taking the bread out of his mouth'. He went to him and struck him sideways with a hurdle. When his victim struggled to his feet, Charles then pulled him by his coat and struck him a blow in the eye with his fist. He said that if he found out that his competitor had asked for the job, he would drop in on to him and give him a good thrashing. Way to go, Charlie!

Here are two news reports that feature Preston and its folk: There was a great blizzard on the night of 27 March 1916. George Jackson (63) of Heath Farm, Breachwood Green (who had a history of heart problems) had been to Hitchin market. Jackson climbed into his trap at 18.40 to return home. He commented to the coachman of the Sun Hotel, 'It's a very rough night but I will have to face it' and was wished a safe journey. At 19.30, postman Ben Norgan approached the crossroads by *Keepers Cottage* and 'saw something black in the road'. It was an overturned trap with its horse standing beside it in a foot of snow. He found only a man's hat and a cushion. He rushed to *The Chequers* at Preston and enlisted the help of its landlord, William Claxton, and farm labourer, Frank Wray. When they returned to the scene, they lifted the trap and found Jackson's body. A medical examination showed that the cause of death was likely a fractured skull. At the inquest (held at Preston's Club House), the coroner commented on the dangerous state of the road where the accident took place. The accident lived long in local minds. It was recalled by Jessie Sansom in *Memories of a Whitwell Woman* with the embellishment that the 'pony had stood buried in the snow all night'.

Frank Brown, a hay and straw dealer who lived at *Sadleir's End,* made several appearances before local courts, but none were as bizarre as the case brought against him by Hannah Frost in 1887 for breach of promise. Brown was a widower with four young children and Hannah (24) had moved in with him as his housekeeper in 1884. Two years later Brown seduced her. When he was informed she was pregnant, he promised to marry her, even getting a licence, but the day before the marriage, he refused to go to the church. Hannah moved out. A little later, Brown said he would be married on the following Saturday or 'he would forfeit his life'. However, on the wedding morning, a little girl came to Hannah's house to say that as it was snowing, the weather was too rough for him to go to the church. Brown still avowed that he wanted to marry her but if he did, he could not pay the costs of this case as he would be 'very much pressed and it would only make the marriage miserable'. (Brown had a track record of baulking at paying courts costs.) He would marry Hannah that moment....but he could not pay the costs and would only marry her if *she* paid them. The jury assessed damages against Brown of £150. The matter was speedily resolved. The court costs were paid by someone and a week later, using his previously-obtained licence, Brown married the heavily-pregnant Hannah at St Mary, Hitchin. Making sure that Frank 'did the right thing', were Hannah's mother, Hannah Frost snr, and Brown's immediate neighbour, Mary Marriott.

If these examples have whetted your interest in local news stories, scores of them in their entirety can be found on the Preston History web site

Acknowledgements

The Preston History web site and this book would not have been possible without the kind help of several local residents and interested, good-natured folk: Benedict Fenwick, Chris Newell, Mary Cave-Brown, Roz Welch, Penny Causer, Kurt Ganzl, Meta Reeves, Harry Hollingsworth, Christina Clews, Robert Freebody, Friedhelm Partenheimer, Ann Fenton, Sam Soto, Jenny Mason, Valerie Holland, Willie Cross, Richard Seebohm, James Bentall of PHC, Betty Palmer, Jane Cole, Hazel L'Abraham, Will Phillips of Buckinghamshire County Museum Resource Centre, the staff of Hertfordshire Archives and Local Studies (especially, Sue Flood), Keith Fitzpatrick-Matthews, Ian Friel, David Hodges of Hitchin Museum, Joseph Elders, Mike Kellard, Jo-Anne Duncan, Maggie Whitby, Robert Sunderland, Rodney Wray, Ron Powney, Howard Trinder, Gordon Wray, Thomas Pickles, Peter Meadows, Marion Gallacher, Graham Scott, Dennis Smith, Tony Swain, Wendy Carey, Eric Peters, Marlene Langley, Val Holland, Alison Brooks have all been particularly helpful and co-operative.

I want to give special mentions to Liz Hunter for her interest, support and help (sometimes candid!) for almost a decade and Wendy Dinsdale (just for being Wendy). Finally, though through clenched teeth, I say a 'Big thanks!' to my long suffering, long-standing friend, Alan Whitby who (in his own words) poof-read the manuscript. After reading every word of this book he muttered the much appreciated comment - 'I'd like to visit Preston sometime'.

References

History of Hitchin (two volumes) - Reginald Hine
The Early History of Temple Dinsley - Reginald Hine
Hitchin Worthies - Reginald Hine
Highways and Byways in Hertfordshire - Herbert W Tompkins (1913)
The Royal Manor of Hitchin - Wentworth Huyshe
Victorian County History - Hertfordshire
History of Hertfordshire - Robert Clutterbuck
Historical Antiquities of Hertfordshire - Sir H Chauncey
The History of Hertfordshire M N Salmon (1728)
The Knights Templar - Helen Nicholson
The Knights Templar - Dr Evelyn Lord
The Manor House of Temple Dinsley - R P Mander
The Origins of Hertfordshire - Prof T Williamson (2000)
The Writings of Nina Freebody, Back Lane, Preston
The Place Names of Hertfordshire - J E B Glover (1936)
The Penguin Translation of the Domesday Book - Prof G H Martin (2002)
Handbook to Hitchin and the Neighbourhood - C Bishop
History of Hertfordshire - J E Cussans
Stagenhoe and the Spanish Countess who Dipped into Spiritualism - R J Pilgram
The History of Stagenhoe - Reginald Hine (1936)
Hitchin and its Neighbourhood - WE Griggs
The manorial records of Dinsley, Maidencroft and Missenden.
The censuses: 1801 - 1911.
Hitchin Rate Books: 1732 - 1845.
Hitchin, Ippollitts and Preston Electoral Registers
The Preston Scrapbook (1953) - Mrs A Maybrick
Emily Soldene - Kurt Ganzl
The Life and Secrets of Almina Carnarvon - Willie Cross
Room does not allow for more details. Should the reader want specific references, please contact the author at p.wray@hotmail.co.uk

Index

Allotments 52
Almina, Countess of Carnarvon 35
Andrews, Stephen Charles 74
Anstruther, Mrs 8
Armstrong family 94
Armstrong, Henry James 74
Ashton, (Charles) Stephen 74
Ashton, Tom 102
Back Lane cottages 63
Ball, Ernest 73
Balliol family 3 - 4, 9
Barrington-White, James and Mrs 6, 30, 56
Benefit Clubs 53
Best kept Herts. Village 55
Biles, Charles Arthur 75
Boreham, Arthur Robert 75
Bradden, Henry 44, 46
Brand, Henry 6, 26
Brown: Frank, 105; William 39
Bryant's map of Herts. 11
Bull Inn, Gosmore 40
Bunyan, John 19
Bunyan's Chapel 26 - 27, 61, 93
Bunyans Cottage 19, 25, 89
Bunyans Dell 19, 105
Burton, Sidney Charles 74
Carter, A 74
Castle Farm 2, 4, 43, 47, 51, 69, 105
Chalkley, Arthur 72
Charlton 1, 7
Chequers Cottages 34, 66, 94 - 98
Chequers Inn 25, 43 - 44, 105
Chequers Lane 64
Claxton, William 75
Club House 58
Cook, Rebecca 77 - 82
Council houses, Chequers Lane 71, 92
Crabbe, Henry 24
Crawley, Arthur Robert 75
Cricket 55
Crunnells Green 16, 50, 63
Crunnells Green House 34 - 35, 50
Crunnells Green Cottage 30
Cullum, William Frederick 76
Cunnells Green (cottages) 34
Curling, Robert 66
Currell, Thomas and Mary 43, 46 - 47, 83 - 84
Darton family 21 -25, 36, 50, 57 - 58, 68
Dawson, Reginald 35, 55
de Kendale family 9, 15
Dead Womans Lane 10, 12, 51
Dennistoun, Ian 35
Dew, John 50
Dinsley Castle 2 - 4, 22
Dinsley Furnival 15
Doomsday Book 2 - 3, 9 - 10, 15
Dower House (see The Cottage)
Downman, Rev E.A. 4
Effigy, Purbeck 3, 6
Elstow, the nuns of 7

English Civil War 16
Evershed, Percy 72
Ewington, William James 72
Fairey, George 45
Farey, Martin Henry 73
Fenton, Ann 76
Fenwicks, Herbert and Violet family 31, 33
Fig Tree Cottage 59
Flint, Jack 53
Foreman, Edward 83
Foster brothers 19, 27, 69
Freebody, Nina 11, 13 - 14, 86
Garner, George William 76
Garner, John 76
Gentle's Cottage 61
Glover, J.E.B. 3, 13
Goldsmith, Oliver, *The Deserted Village* 14
Gootheridge, John 51, 70
Gosmore 1, 4, 49
Grey, Edwin 42, 46
Griggs, W. E. 49
Hall family, Samuel, Lily and Dorothy 92
Halsey, Thomas 25
Harper, Harry Edward 73
Harwood, Thomas 21
Hayden, Joseph 23
Hey, David 47
Hill End 34
Hinde, Robert and Mrs 4, 22 - 23, 49
Hine, Reginald 1, 4 , 6 - 8, 10, 16, 18 - 19, 49, 105
Hitchwood 1, 79
Hitchwood Cottages 30, 34
Holly Cottages 66, 89
Home Farm 70
Horn, Pamela 37
Horse and Groom Inn 44
Hughes, Richard 81
Hunsdon House (see Castle Farm)
Hunter, Liz 14, 86
Huyshe, Wentworth 2 - 3, 5, 8
I'Anson, William Barker 73
Ippollitts 1
Ithell, Benedict family 20 - 21, 49
Jeeves, William 44
Jenkins, William 73
Jekyll, Gertrude 31, 33
Keepers Cottage 89
Kenwood Cottage 58
Kiln Wood 1
Kiln Wood Cottage 34
King Henry VIII 15
King Stephen 5
Kings Walden 1, 7, 47, 53
Knights Hospitaller 8, 10, 15
Knights Templar 1 - 10
Laburnum Lodge (aka Joyners Cottage) 58
Ladygrove Farm 34, 104
Land Girls 80
Langley End House 34

Index

Langley End House 34
Latchmore, T.W. 18
Line's Cottage 61
Lord, Evelyn 7, 10
Luyens, Sir Edwin 31 - 34
Macmillan, Frederick 27 - 28
Maidencroft, manor of 15
Maybrick, Frederick and Ann 37, 70, 86, 99
Middleditch, Dick and Ethel 89
Minsden Chapel 5 - 6, 9, 16 - 18
Minsden, manor 9
Morality 46
Murphy, John 76
Newell family 95
O'Donnell, Elliott 18
Offley Holes Farm 16, 67
Offley Holes House 67, 91
Old Forge, The 60, 100
Palmer, Arthur James 74
Payne, Ernest 76
Peters' Cottage 59
Peters family 37, 43, 54, 59, 100 - 101
Peters, Christopher Thomas 76
Peters, Edward 75
Peters, Henry George 74
Peters, Walter Charles 74
Plague (Black Death) 10, 13
Plaiting Schools 37, 42
Pond Farm 2, 69
Powell, John Thomas 73
Poynders End Farm 26, 30
Poynders End Farm
Preceptory chapel 3, 5, 7, 9
Preston Castle (see DinsleyCastle)
Preston Farm 67
Preston Green 2, 55 - 56
Preston Hill 1, 48, 83
Preston Hill Farm 2, 47, 70, 90, 94, 104
Preston Hill 'murder' case 83
Preston House 62
Preston Pound 50
Preston Schools 28, 36 - 37, 42, 52, 84 - 85
Preston Scrapbook 99
Preston Well 57
Princess Helena College 7, 33, 36, 55, 68, 77, 79, 81
Prior of Wymondley 3 - 4
Pryor family, (Henry, Ralson and Geoffrey) 26 - 28, 44, 52, 55
Pryor House, aka *The Laburnums* 39, 59
Raffell, Jack 40
Red Lion 39 - 40, 93
Reed, John William 73
Reeves Cottage 63, 90, 104
Robinson, Frederick 59
Rose Cottage 65
Sadleir family 15 - 16, 67
Sadleirs End 65
Salmon, Nathaniel 3
Saunderson, Joseph and Harriet 39
Scarbrow, Ray 40

School Lane Bungalows 35
Scott family, 'Will' and Ethel 93
Seebohm, Derek and Hugh 30, 91
Sharp family: Herbert, 56; Percy, 76; Sidney, 72
Shaw, Frederick 76
Sims, Algernon William 76
Skeat, The Rev. Professor 3
Smith, Leonard Charles 76
Smith, Sidney 76
Sootfield Green 41, 43, 66, 91
Spindle Cottage 64
St Albans Highway 9, 51, 56, 70
St Martin's Church, Preston 6, 28 - 30, 93
St Martins Place 60
St Mary's Church, Hitchin 9, 16 - 17, 20, 23
Stagenhoe 7, 10, 13
Stagenhoe House 6 - 7
Stanley, 'Bill' and Rose 98
Stanley, Peter 79
Stevens, Simon 36
Strawplaiting 41 - 43
Sugden, Flossie 103
Sunderland, Robert 14, 79, 81 - 82, 90 - 91
Swain family 39
Swain, John 76
Swain, William 75
Swedish Houses, Chequers Lane 70
Tatmore Hills Lane 11 - 12
Templars Lane 70
Temple Clock 27
Temple Dinsley 1 - 10, 15 - 16, 20 - 28, 31 - 33, 35 - 36
Temple Dinsley, Rose Garden 33
Temple Farm 26, 70
The Cottage, the aka *The Dower House* 25, 27, 68
Thomas, Frank 79
Tomkins, Herbert W 6
Vickers, Douglas 31, 35, 44, 55, 61, 69
Vickers, Oliver Henry 76
Victorian County History 2, 5, 10
Vine Cottage 59, 98
Wabey, Samuel 83 - 84
Wain Wood 1, 13, 19
Walkden, John Henry 77
Walker, Frederick 76
Wallers, 'Bert' and Dennis and families 86 - 87
Wayley (see Welei)
Wedelee 2
Weeks, John 25, 27
Welei 10 - 14, 91
Wessex Saddleback pigs 35, 69
Wilderness, The 65, 88
Wilkinson, Prof. Tom 1, 11
Woodhams, Mary and Bill 84 - 85
Woodrow, Frederick 74, 77
World War Two 77 - 82
Wray family: Bob, 54, 75; Ernest, 73; Frank, 75; Charles, 105; Charlie, 75; Alfred and Emily 96 - 98; Flossie, 103; Sam and Grace, 104
Wright, George 45, 51, 70
Young, John 44